Inspirations for Daily Living

WALLIS C. METTS

LARRY JAMES PEACOCK

RANDY PETERSEN

PUBLICATIONS INTERNATIONAL, LTD.

Wallis C. Metts, Ph.D., chairs the department of communication at Spring Arbor College in Spring Arbor, Michigan. His published works have appeared in over thirty periodicals including *Christianity Today, Moody Monthly,* and *Guideposts for Kids Magazine.* He has a Ph.D. in interdisciplinary studies (English, communication, and religious studies) from Michigan State University and is the co-author of *Children's Book of the Bible.*

Larry James Peacock serves as minister of Malibu United Methodist Church in Malibu, California. He writes and publishes *Water Words,* a collection of contemporary worship resources, and his articles appear in such publications as *Alive Now, The Upper Room, Church Worship,* and *Weavings: A Journal of the Christian Spiritual Life.* He frequently leads retreats and spiritual workshops for the Academy for Spiritual Formation.

Randy Petersen studied ancient languages at Wheaton College before becoming executive editor of *Bible Newsletter* and other publications. Now a full-time freelance writer and editor, he has contributed to more than twenty books, including *The Revell Bible Dictionary* and the *Christian Book of Lists,* as well as to a wide variety of magazines, including *Christian History.* Mr. Petersen is the co-author of the book *Jesus: His Life and Times.*

Photo credits:

Front cover: **David Olsen/Tony Stone Images**

Back cover: **Darrell Gulin/Tony Stone Images**

Noella Ballenger: 71, 163, 166, 203; **Ed Cooper Photo:** 11, 15, 27, 29, 31, 33, 44, 47, 49, 51, 57, 62, 75, 79, 82, 85, 86, 87, 109, 111, 113, 114, 127, 157, 161, 169, 177, 187, 190, 193, 200, 202, 211, 213, 220, 224, 225, 229, 239, 244, 251, 253, 261, 275, 280, 291, 308, 317; **Kent & Donna Dannen:** 219, 283; **FPG International:** Bruce Byers: 309; Frank Cezus: 158; Walter Choroszewski: 155; Louis Goldman: 189; Dennis Hallinan: 24; L'Image Magick, Inc.: 277; David McGlynn: 249; James McLoughlin: 120; Christian Michaels: 313; Edmund Nagele: 16; Richard T. Nowitz: 181; Stan Osolinski: 134; Cindy Pitou: 55; Renaud Thomas: 59; Arthur Tilley: 91; **International Stock:** Doug Campbell: 311; Bob Jacobson: 143; **Santokh Kochar Photography:** 129, 292; **Richard T. Nowitz:** 48, 74, 182, 302; **Lee Snider/Photo Images:** 215; **Tony Stone Images:** Paul Chesley: 105; Chad Ehlers: 233; Liz Hymans: 9; George Lepp: 271; David Muench: 258; Pat O'Hara: Table of contents (center), 67; David Olsen: End sheets; Michael Orton: 23; Richard Passmore: 89; Ryan & Beyer: 153; Andy Sacks: 133; Tim Thompson: 295; Darryl Torckler: 173; Jean-Marc Truchet: 137; Larry Ulrich: 207, 269; Greg Vaughn: 37; **SuperStock:** 17, 19, 20, 25, 28, 35, 41, 41, 45, 52, 60, 61, 65, 69, 73, 94, 95, 98, 99, 117, 123, 139, 141, 151, 160, 165, 176, 178, 196, 212, 216, 243, 262, 266, 303, 307.

CONTENTS

INTRODUCTION

*Now I am about to go the way of all the earth. You know
with all your heart and soul that not one of all the good
promises the Lord your God gave you has failed. Every promise
has been fulfilled; not one has failed.*

JOSHUA 23:14, NIV

ON A COOL summer evening long, long ago, an aging warrior gathered the elders of his tribe together on a mountainside in central Palestine. Joshua had been their captain in a successful series of battles, claiming the land around them as their inheritance, promised to their father Abraham by Jehovah—the God of Israel. Now Joshua was old and tired—and hopeful.

His people had been through many difficulties, but now there was peace. After experiencing famine and slavery, they had wandered in the wilderness for 40 years. Then, under Joshua's leadership and with God's help, they fought their way into the mountains their forefathers had left almost 400 years earlier.

On the eve of Joshua's death, the land was theirs, but many political and religious enemies surrounded them. Joshua warned them of these dangers. He reminded them to love their God and to obey him.

He also encouraged them, with a statement both simple and sincere. "Not one of all the good promises the Lord your God gave you has failed," he reminded them. "Every promise has been fulfilled." This truth had sustained them in their struggles, and he expected it would continue to do so.

He was right. Three thousand years later his people have sustained unspeakable horrors, including the holocaust. But they have stayed together, in exile and under every sort of difficulty, because they continued to believe the promises of their God. As their second and greatest king, David, said in one of his prayers to God, "Your promises have been thoroughly tested, and your servant loves them" (Psalm 119:140, NIV).

Christians have since joined them in this love, finding comfort and strength in the many promises that God pledged in the Bible. Speaking of the Scriptures, the Apostle Peter wrote: "Through these he has given us his very great and precious promises, so that through them you may participate in the divine nature" (2 Peter 1:4, NIV).

This book will help you discover many of these promises and claim them for your own, so that you too may participate in the divine nature. Through meditations, anecdotes, poems, hymns, and ancient prayers, you will look at these old promises in new ways.

There is much to discover. You will be reminded of his steadfast love, which enables us to be called the children of God. You will consider the promise of his presence in everything from the mundane to the miraculous. You will find hope to strengthen your heart. With the psalmist, you may even shout for joy—or at least hum a tune of thanksgiving.

The Bible is filled with reassurances that God comforts us and strengthens us. He can turn our mourning into dancing and our weaknesses into strength. The list goes on and on. God promises forgiveness. He promises to hear our prayers. He promises us abundant life now and eternal life later.

The Bible says his ways are "unsearchable," far beyond our ability to fathom. But as you understand his promises you will understand him better, and you will catch a fresh glimpse of his character. His promises show us that he is gracious and compassionate, full of mercy and truth. His promises show us that he is majestic and mysterious, filled with holy passion and power. Most of all, his promises show us that he is faithful, and has been faithful, not just to the patriarchs and the apostles, but to each of us, right down to this day.

The writers of this book have all experienced his faithfulness. Although they represent different ages, occupations, and interests, they have seen and believed these promises of hope.

As you read, you will bring your own perspective to the promises collected and considered in this book. You will be reminded of God's faithfulness to you and to the people you love. You will be encouraged and blessed as you see God's presence in the ordinary events of your day and in the darkest days of your life. In every circumstance, God's promises encourage us and give us hope.

In a world filled with cynicism and despair, hope is a good thing. It is the joyful expectation that God will do what he says he will do. It is the confidence that he is in control, and that he is full of compassion. His promises are not platitudes; they are powerful statements of who he is and what he does. And they are true.

GOD PROMISES HOPE

I WAIT FOR THE Lord, my soul waits, and in his word I hope; my soul waits for the Lord more than those who watch for the morning, more than those who watch for the morning. O Israel, hope in the Lord! For with the Lord there is steadfast love, and with him is great power to redeem.

PSALM 130:5–7

DOING THE IMPOSSIBLE

*Jesus looked at them and said, "With mortals it is impossible,
but for God all things are possible."*

MATTHEW 19:26

ROM OUR PERSPECTIVE, a lot of things look tough. There is the responsibility of maintaining a long-term commitment to our spouse and children, even on days when they aren't exactly endearing. There is the responsibility of dealing fairly and kindly with our coworkers, even when our boss is being a jerk and our peers are self-absorbed and mean-spirited. And then there is God's expectation that we will put him first in our lives.

Practically impossible, we say. But Jesus said we don't have to do everything by ourselves; in fact, with God's help we can do the inconceivable. With "God all things are possible," Jesus said.

He said this in the context of something that was difficult for his disciples to even imagine. A young man had come to him and asked how to get eternal life. This was no ordinary young man, however. He was a young man of privilege and responsibility. He had gone to good schools, come from a good home, and done many good things. He was rich and devout, the model of Jewish propriety.

Jesus did not answer his question with any doctrinal formulation nor with any calming reassurance that he was on the right track. Instead he got to the heart of the matter. "Go, sell your possessions, and give the money to the poor," he said. "Then come, follow me."

The young man could not or would not do this. The Bible says, "He went away grieving, because he had many possessions."

Jesus was not really saying that we have to give away everything we own to have eternal life. For a different young man with a different set of circumstances he may have suggested something different. Jesus needed to know what the young man loved most, and his request was a simple but effective test.

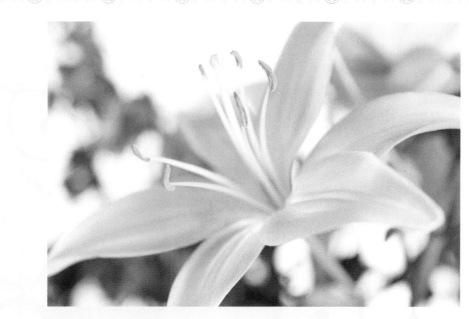

The disciples were amazed. If this young man could not get into heaven, who could? Like most of us, they were impressed by what they saw on the outside. In fact, their culture taught them that wealth was a sure sign of God's blessing.

But God is interested in our hearts, and so Jesus said something that seemed very odd to them, and even to us. He said it was easier for a camel to go through the eye of a needle than for a rich man to get into heaven, a startling image to say the least.

If a rich man can't get into heaven, who then can be saved, the disciples asked. That's when Jesus said, "For mortals it is impossible, but for God all things are possible." And then he began to explain what the kingdom of God is really like, a place where "the first will be last" (Matthew 20:16).

What Jesus promises is God's help for difficult things: not just physically difficult things, like going through the eye of a needle, but emotionally and spiritually difficult challenges as well. Sometimes it is hard to know God, or love God, or believe God. But he can and does give us what we need to do just that. Because with God, nothing is impossible.

Dear God,
Help me to trust you for the
impossible. Thank you for
confidence and courage, not just
to do the right things but to
believe the right things, too.
Amen.

A Prayer by St. Paul

For this reason I bow my knees before the Father, from whom every family in heaven and on earth takes its name. I pray that, according to the riches of his glory, he may grant that you be strengthened in your inner being with power through his Spirit, and that Christ may dwell in your hearts through faith, as you are being rooted and grounded in love. I pray that you may have the power to comprehend, with all the saints what is the breadth and length and height and depth, and to know the love of Christ that surpasses knowledge, so that you may be filled with all the fullness of God. Now to him who by the power at work within us is able to accomplish abundantly far more than all we can ask or imagine, to him be glory in the church and in Christ Jesus to all generations, for ever and ever. Amen.

Ephesians 3:14–21

A CANDLE OF HOPE

I know the plans I have for you, says the Lord, plans for your welfare and not for harm, to give you a future with hope.

JEREMIAH 29:11

A FRIEND WAS WORKING on a writing assignment that involved a trip to Columbia, South America, to research the underground world of drugs. It was a difficult and frightening experience, and when he came back to the United States to write the story, the darkness seemed to have followed him home. During our prayer time in Sunday worship, his wife would request prayers for him, asking that we hold him in the light of Jesus, who is the light of the world. One day when he went out to get his mail, he found a candle in his mailbox. It was a turning point in his work; he knew there was a special light all around him—people who cared for him. He found hope to complete an important project.

"I know the plans I have for you . . . to give you a future with hope." Often God works in unassuming human deeds. Our sense of hope in the future may not come with lightning bolts or grand plans. It may be as simple as a candle in the mailbox, or it may come in countless other ways: an unexpected call from a friend just after we have received bad news from a doctor; an offer of help in organizing a letter-writing campaign to protect the environment; a parent who holds on to the bike again and again until a child can master the two-wheeler. It may be a word or a hug, a letter or a community protest—but we see the possibilities in the future, and we are filled with hope.

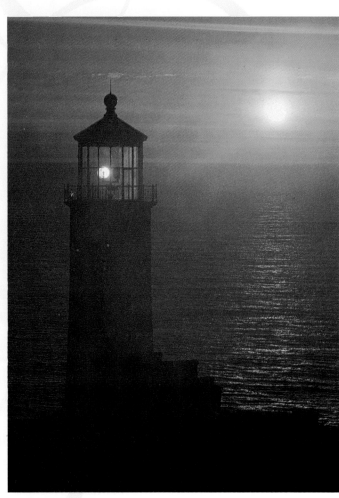

Hope is one of God's great works. It comes as a gift. It is not something that we earn. It comes through the actions of others, but it also comes more mysteriously, as a whisper in the night, a dawning clarity of direction, or a sudden burst of confidence. God is looking out for the welfare of all creation, and hope is given to people in all times and places, in all situations and circumstances. Though we may wonder how

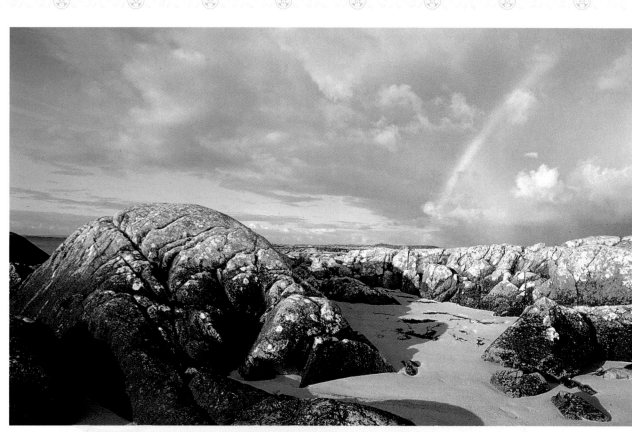

long it will take for the "future with hope" to come about, we are not to doubt the outcome. "I know the plans I have for you . . . a future with hope." As some friends in an African-American church once told me, "God may not come when you want, but God always comes on time."

The promise of Jeremiah finds a resting place deep inside us, reminding us that God is still at work in and through us and the people around us. God is working for good in our lives; he is especially at work in the midst of anyone who is struggling to find food, shelter, and basic human rights. Patience and persistence are often companions of hope. God takes a long view of history, and he faithfully works to bring in the new reign of peace and freedom. We are never alone in our hope for a new day.

We hope not just in ourselves or our own resources, though such confidence in our God-given gifts is an important factor, but we hope in God. He is a God who sends rainbows after rain, joy out of sorrow, and turns Good Friday deaths into Easter resurrections. God promises a future with hope, and God is with us now with plans, patience, and persistence. He is working to bring in a glorious future for all the people of the earth.

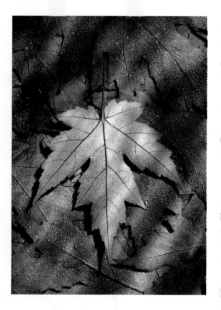

Optimism and hope are radically different attitudes. Optimism is the expectation that things—the weather, human relationships, the economy, the political situation, and so on—will get better. Hope is the trust that God will fulfill God's promises to us in a way that leads us to true freedom. The optimist speaks about concrete changes in the future. The person of hope lives in the moment with the knowledge and trust that all of life is in good hands.

HENRI NOUWEN, *BREAD FOR THE JOURNEY: A DAYBOOK OF WISDOM AND FAITH*

WORTH THE WAIT

For in hope we are saved. Now hope that is seen is not hope.
For who hopes for what is seen? But if we hope for what
we do not see, we wait for it with patience.

ROMANS 8:24–25

KIM THINKS JULY will never come. She's pregnant and due in the middle of summer, just a few months away. Some women glow when they're with child; not Kim. She's having a rough time of it. Her body has just gone berserk. She's hot and cold, tired and always hungry; her clothes don't fit right; even her fingers feel fat. Then she keeps hearing about the hours of labor she'll have to go through to bear this child.

How does she get through it all? By imagining what it will be like to hold her baby in her arms. That will make everything worthwhile.

That's the exact picture the Apostle Paul paints in Romans 8. The whole universe is suffering labor pains right now, and we are, too, but we await the birth of a great new day that will be well worth the wait.

Not everyone shares that hope. Take a good look at the human condition these days; it's easy to get dragged down into despair. Peace talks fall apart; kids are gunning down other kids; terrorists wreak havoc. Where is God when you need him?

In Samuel Beckett's absurdist play *Waiting for Godot*, two men spend their time "blathering in the void," waiting for a mysterious acquaintance who keeps promising to show up but never does.

"Let's go."

"We can't."

"Why not?"

"We're waiting for Godot."

Many people feel they've been waiting for God with the same results. Nothing. They're dealing with disease, bad relationships, or depression, and they've been praying for miracles for years, but

God seems not to pay attention. The difficulties remain.

In the face of these cold realities, the message of Romans 8 is defiantly cheerful: Don't give up hope. The best is yet to come. This is no Pollyanna, pie-in-the-sky platitude. This is more than Little Orphan Annie singing, "Tomorrow, tomorrow, I luv ya, tomorrow!" The preceding verses acknowledge that the whole universe is "groaning"; it's locked in a pattern of decay, tearing

its heart out while yearning for restoration. It's definitely tough out there, but there's glory ahead. God has a plan. His people will be rescued from their suffering, and the whole created order will be set right.

That's the hope we have, and that hope keeps us going. Hope is relentlessly future tense. It's always next time, next season, that next big promotion. When we get what we have hoped for, we don't have to hope for it anymore. As long as we're locked on this treadmill of time, we need hope to keep us moving forward. Hopelessness kills; hope saves. Someday God will stop the treadmill in its tracks, reversing the process of death and decay, re-creating the world in wonder and glory.

Meanwhile, we "wait with patience."

It makes you wonder if the apostle had Psalm 40 echoing in his head: "I waited patiently for the Lord; he

JUST A THOUGHT

In The Inferno, *Dante pictures an inscription over the gates of Hell: "Abandon hope, all ye who enter here." But it might be said that those who cross that portal have already abandoned hope long before then. Hope allows us to open our eyes to God, who redeems us.*

inclined to me and heard my cry. He drew me up from the desolate pit, out of the miry bog . . . " God fulfills our hopes in a million little ways every day. Someday he'll do it in a great big way. Won't that be something?

"You are his child."
The Spirit calls, he's calling you!
"You are his child."
Hear him now, he's telling you.

We groan with all creation,
Waiting for his call.
Groaning for liberation,
The redemption of us all.

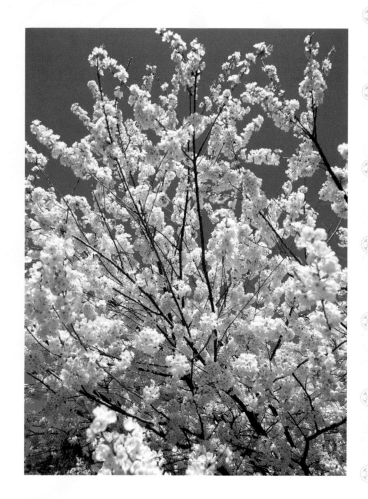

The Spirit knows we are weak,
But he knows how to pray,
And he'll sweetly intercede
When we don't know what to say.

He knows the suffering's tough
And the waiting is long,
But he promises glory for us
And this hoping makes us strong.

THE POWER OF HOPE

May the God of hope fill you with all joy and peace in believing,
so that you may abound with hope by the power of the Holy Spirit.
ROMANS 15:13

GOING TO FUNERALS is an occasional social obligation that makes me feel uncomfortable. I'm not afraid to die, or at least I don't think I am, but I am afraid of not being able to feel the pain of those who have lost a family member.

I remember going to the funeral for the mother of a friend at work. He and I shared an office one year, and I was glad to be able to represent our community of coworkers. But I felt, as I often do, like a mere observer, not a participant.

The funeral director, like most funeral directors, was sober and unobtrusive. The organ played "It Will Be Worth It All When We See Jesus," and everyone was quiet. The whirring of the ceiling fan was the only other noise as the pastor asked God to give us "reverent and submissive hearts."

A son-in-law offered an eulogy. It was a tribute to a woman who, after 44 years of marriage and three years as a widow, left a son and a daughter and grandchildren who loved her and love each other—no small accomplishment. Then a granddaughter read a poem: "We gripped your finger, but we really held your heart." The audience began to stir.

Then Tom stood up and talked about his mom and what she believed. I'm not sure I could do that—speak at my own mother's funeral. But he did, and he did it well. He talked dry-eyed about the grace of God and how it had sustained her. He said he looked forward to seeing her again. Then he sat down and cried like a baby.

I realized then that the faith expressed that day was not a crutch for emotionally unstable people. It was a simple but painful celebration of God's promise that death is swallowed up in victory and that we will see our loved ones again.

That's hope, and hope in this sense is not just wishful thinking. It is the confident expectation that God is in control, and that he intends good for us. Hope is at the heart of our faith, and it distinguishes believers from unbelievers.

Even at a funeral we expect God to do the wise thing, the right thing, the best thing. We know he will come and set things right, if not in this life then in the next. We may have our heartbreaks here, but ultimately we expect freshness and radiance in God's presence.

We are full of joy and peace, and our hearts "overflow with hope."

Lord,
I gladly put my hope in you.
You are all the things your
Word says you are: my
strength, my shield, my
salvation.
In a world filled with darkness
and doubt, I expect you to
refresh me with your light and
give me joy.
Amen.

O MASTER, LET ME WALK WITH THEE

In hope that sends a shining ray
far down the future's broad'ning way,
in peace that only thou canst give,
with thee, O Master, let me live.

WASHINGTON GLADDEN

WE TRUST

I falter where I firmly trod,

And falling with my weight of cares

Upon the great world's altar stairs

That slope through darkness up to God,

I stretch lame hands of faith, and grope,

And gather dust and chaff, and call

To what I feel is Lord of all,

And faintly trust the larger hope.

ALFRED, LORD TENNYSON

TAKE HEART, BE HOPEFUL

Be strong, and let your heart take courage,
all you who wait for the Lord.

PSALM 31:24

FRIEND OF MINE wrote a song called "Be Brave." My friend has a big strong voice, and when he sings the song I feel tears come to my eyes. I feel wonderfully hopeful and encouraged. I love the song; he mixes individual bravery and a "light" that comes from outside us and shines on us. Some days I feel strong and look forward to facing the world, but other days I have to count on a courage that comes from beyond me.

The psalmist is likewise telling the Hebrews to keep their focus on the Lord, to a strength beyond themselves. The psalmist recognizes that the people have a strength that can be encouraged, but he ends the psalm with the deeper strength of the Lord.

There is another biblical passage that talks of "taking heart," of having courage in the circumstances of life. Jesus and his disciples are moving through Jericho when a blind beggar yells out, "Jesus, Son of David, have mercy on me" (Mark 10:47). He yells again, even though people are trying to shut him up. Jesus says, "Call him here." The crowd turns to the beggar and says, "Take heart; get up, he is calling you." So the man gets up, leaves his begging cloak behind, goes to Jesus, and is healed. The words of the psalmist echo through this passage. The people who have been waiting and hoping—have been strong—are invited to rise up and come to Jesus, who brings healing and hope.

To be strong may not be a matter of physical strength but rather an orientation toward God, who gives us incredible courage in the face of a world that is often filled with fear and violence. To be strong is to know that Jesus is calling, that God is coming, that hope rests in God.

I begin my mornings with a time of prayer and meditation, a time of waiting on the Lord. I pray for God's presence, asking for courage, and, because God promises to be with me in all circumstances, I have hope. I can go through each day hopeful and with confidence that God will guide me, help me, support me, challenge me.

While optimism makes us live as if someday soon things will go better for us, hope frees us from the need to predict the future and allows us to live in the present, with the deep trust that God will never leave us alone but will fulfill the deepest desires of our heart.

HENRI NOUWEN,
HERE AND NOW

Recently a woman asked if she could write a play for our church. She showed me some of her other writing, and I said "yes." When she brought me a script, it did not fit our needs. I worried how to tell her. I did not feel strong-hearted, but in my morning time I asked God for courage. I hoped my meeting with the author would be blessed. It turned out she was glad for more direction. She had been cautious in her first attempt, and she was eager to do better.

Be strong, let your heart take courage, and trust in the Lord.

YOUTH AND CONSEQUENCES

For you, O Lord, are my hope, my trust, O Lord, from my youth.

PSALM 71:5

"IS THAT ALL THERE IS?"

In Peggy Lee's tribute to disappointment, all sorts of childhood hopes are dashed, and there's nothing left to do but keep dancing.

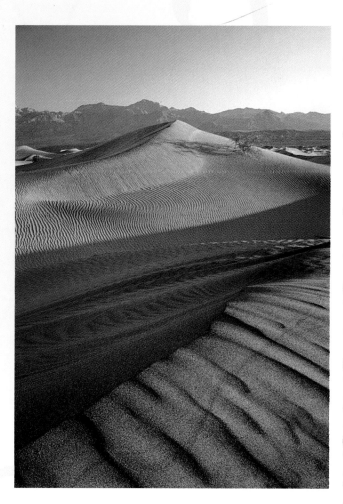

For all too many, that's the story of their lives. They grew up believing, trusting, hoping, but then adulthood struck them like a cement truck. They had a painful romance, and they've stopped believing in love. They studied science or philosophy, and they've stopped trusting God. They got stuck in a dead-end job, and they've stopped hoping for the future.

"Is that all there is?"

The psalmist sings praises to God as his "hope," indicating that he has trusted the Lord since he was young. It's not surprising that he trusted God as a child, since children tend to be trusting. It's more amazing that he's still trusting God as an adult. Didn't he ever have his faith shaken? Didn't he ever face disillusionment that made him lose his religion?

The previous verse puts the psalmist in "the grasp of the unjust and cruel." Things are not going well for him, but he maintains his hope in God. Maybe you've heard of "tough love." This is tough hope.

People have the idea that faith is kid stuff. Hope is a sweet outlook for a child, but adults get cynical. "When you know better, boys and girls, you'll stop expecting so much out of life."

Maybe that's why Jesus said we had to become like little children to enter God's kingdom. We need to rub the calluses off our hearts and dare to dream again. In spite of all the pain we've been through, we need to trust in God, who loves us, who will make everything all right, eventually.

And if we take our cue from the psalmist, it's not about philosophy or science; it's not even about our

I am a man of hope because I believe that God is born anew each morning, because I believe that he is creating the world at this very moment. He did not create it at a distant moment in time, then forget about it. It is happening now: we must therefore be ready to expect the unexpected from God.

LEON JOSEPH CARDINAL SUENENS, *SUENENS*

dreams or goals; it's about our personal relationship with God. Note how the psalmist doesn't just say that God gives him hope, though surely he does. No, the Lord is his hope. The believer does not trust in some pretty picture of life here on earth or hereafter but in a living, loving Lord.

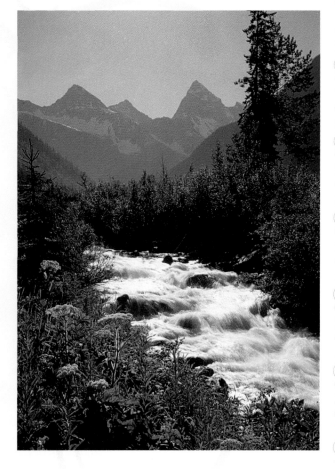

As pants the deer for the cooling streams
when heated in the chase,
so longs my soul, O God, for you,
and your refreshing grace.

I sigh to think of happier days
when you, O Lord, were nigh;
when ev'ry heart was tuned to praise,
and none more blest than I.

Why restless, why cast down, my soul?
Hope still, and you will sing
the praise of him who is your God,
your health's eternal spring.

TATE AND BRADY, HENRY F. LYTE
BASED ON PSALM 42, ADAPTED

NEVER ASHAMED

Uphold me according to your promise, that I may live,
and let me not be put to shame in my hope.

PSALM 119:116

RON IS A CUBS FAN. He discovered baseball as a boy during the summer of 1969. The whole Chicago area was psyched about the Cubs, and they were having a great year. Williams, Santo, Banks, Jenkins—they could go all the way.

They didn't. The Miracle Mets ambushed them. Young Ron was devastated, but he looked forward to the 1970 season. They still had a good team, they could do it. Well, they didn't win the pennant the next year, or the next. In fact, Ron's pushing 40 now, and the Cubs still haven't won. And yet every spring he studies their roster and determines that "this team can win." And every fall, as the cheers die out at Wrigley Field, it's "Wait until next year."

Ron has friends who root for the Braves or the Yankees, and they've had plenty to cheer about. In October, when those teams are in the thick of post-season play, they gloat a bit in Ron's direction. Poor guy, why did he pick such losers to support? And yet Ron is not ashamed of his team. It's just a matter of time. Maybe this year they'll win it all.

The psalmist understands that he's going out on a limb by putting his hope and trust in God. There are plenty of enemies around who are ready to mock him if God doesn't come through. And the Lord's victories sometimes take some time to become obvious. But, like a loyal Cub fan, he reaffirms his commitment, and he begs the Lord not to let him down.

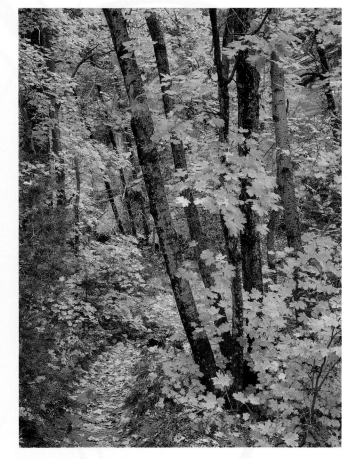

There are plenty of times in our lives when it seems that trusting the Lord is precisely the wrong thing to do. Any sane person would, say, take a higher-paying job rather than a more fulfilling one. It only makes sense to fight for your rights, put yourself first, show people who's boss. No one is totally honest with the IRS, their employer, or their spouse, are they? And the entire advertising industry is designed to make you want more than you have; it would be unpatriotic not to go along with that.

But if we truly put our hope in the Lord—not in money, self, or things—we take a risk. We go against the grain. Others may make fun of us. And it may take a while before the wisdom of our choices becomes clear. We may have to wait until next year—or the next life. But the Lord promises to uphold his people, and he assures us we won't be ashamed.

❋　　❋　　❋　　❋

Hope, like faith, is nothing if it is not courageous;
it is nothing if it is not ridiculous.

THORNTON WILDER

❋　　❋　　❋　　❋

Lord,
You give me hope when I pin my hopes on you.
When the future looks bleak, I seek you,
And you remind me that you're not finished with me yet.
You've got a plan,
Which you'll tell me about on a "need to know" basis.
I can accept that, and
Still, it gives me hope.

Lord,
You prove trustworthy when I trust in you.
When I take a chance on doing what you want
(Instead of what everyone else expects),
You make it work.
Not always right away, this minute—
You leave me hanging sometimes—
But sooner or later I come around to say,
"Hey, that God of mine
Really knows what he's doing!"

Lord,
You give me something to live for,
And so I'll live for you.
I see zombies all around me—
You know, the "living dead"—
They think they're having a blast, but
They're just blasting themselves to oblivion.
You make it all mean something.
You give me a future, a present,
You make sense of my past.
You give me hope.
Thank You.

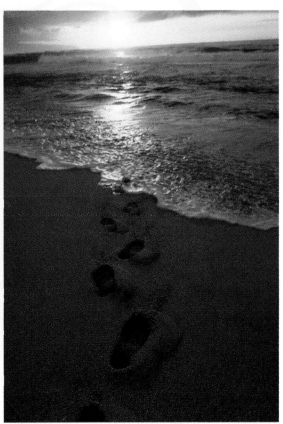

God Promises His Presence

WHERE CAN I GO from your spirit? Or where can I flee from your presence? If I ascend to heaven, you are there; if I make my bed in Sheol, you are there. If I take the wings of the morning and settle at the farthest limits of the sea, even there your hand shall lead me, and your right hand shall hold me fast.

PSALM 139:7–10

GOD KNOWS ME, LOVES ME

I praise you, for I am fearfully and wonderfully made. Wonderful are your works; that I know very well. My frame was not hidden from you, when I was being made in secret, intricately woven in the depths of the earth. Your eyes beheld my unformed substance. In your book were written all the days that were formed for me, when none of them as yet existed.

PSALM 139:14–16

THE SCOPE OF PSALM 139 is as broad as the horizon and as personal as a newborn baby. Take some time to read the whole psalm, and discover a God who knows and cares for you.

I once went on a five-day retreat to a small hermitage run by a couple who would oversee my time of prayer and reflection. I moved into the trailer nestled deep in the woods on their property. I was excited and a little scared to have five days to myself, by myself. I had brought many books to read, and I had some ideas for projects that I might work on. The first night there, Ron came to talk to me about my plans for the retreat. I told him about what I intended to read and do. He gently suggested that I might want to set all the plans aside for the first day and just spend some time reading Psalm 139. I was open to the possibility, though I wanted to get on with my agenda. Ron suggested I be open to God's agenda.

In the morning, I decided to take a walk to check out my new surroundings, eat a leisurely breakfast, and then read Psalm 139 before moving on to my other tasks. I never made it to the other tasks that day, and I never read most of the books I had so carefully packed. I got caught by God addressing me in Psalm 139.

God knows me so well. God knows "when I sit down or when I rise up" (Psalm 139:2). God knows my thoughts and is acquainted with all my ways (verses 2 and 3). God knew when I was being made in secret, knit together in my mother's womb (verses 13 and 15). I was overwhelmed with God's knowledge and presence in my life. I wanted to both praise God and hide from him.

I wanted to praise God for the wonder of my life. "I am wonderfully made." I could take a walk and marvel

at the way my body moved, thrill at the sight of the tall pines, and wonder at the smell of the roses along the trail. I could eat breakfast and enjoy the taste of orange juice; I could turn my head when I heard a peck at the window and discover a cardinal greeting me every morning (sometimes earlier than I wanted to awaken). The five senses are part of being "wonderfully made," and they bring joy to living. But I also wanted to hide from God.

I was a little ashamed to be known so well. I hadn't done anything drastically wrong, but the thought of God knowing all my thoughts, knowing all my words, and watching over all my actions was overwhelming. I was humbled, and I was glad Jesus told us that God is a forgiving God. Even as I was aware of my shortcomings, I was confronted and blessed by a God who knows me so well and still loves me.

There is no place we can go and be out of the presence of God. "Where can I flee from your presence?... If I take the wings of the morning and settle at the farthest limits of the sea, even there your hand shall lead me, and your right hand shall hold me fast" (verses 7, 9–10). The images are so powerful, so comforting. Even before we are born we are known by God, held in God's heart. Humans are wonderfully made, and God looks out for our well being.

I take a walk most mornings. Most people in the neighborhood probably think that I do it for the dog that accompanies me, but I really do it for me. I want to begin each day gently, quietly, so I can sense once again the presence of God. I can read about God's right hand holding me and about being made by God, but I want to try to open myself to remembering and experiencing the presence and love of God. As I walk, I say this prayer: "New every morning is your love, great God of light, and all day long you are working for good in the world. Stir up in us desire to serve you, to live peacefully with our neighbors, and to devote each day to your Son, our Savior, Jesus Christ the Lord. Amen."

The prayer adjusts my focus for the day and puts me in touch with God and God's desire to be present in all the activities of my day. I return home from the walk a little better prepared for the day.

The psalmist reminds us that it is not only our personal efforts that keep us open to God, but that God is continually seeking to be present to us. "Wonderful are

your works, that I know very well." You do not have to read many psalms to know that creation is one of the ways that God is present to us. The stars, the sun, the trees, indeed, even the "heavens are telling the glory of God" (Psalm 19:1). The glories of creation not only points us toward the Creator, but they become metaphors for our spiritual journey. The fast moving stream reminds me of how fast my life is going, and that I need to find still waters for rest. The winter trees remind me that even in emptiness work is being done to prepare for the spring. The beauty inside a tulip calls me to look deep inside myself and others for the traces of God's gifts. These works of God are wonderful teachers.

I don't remember the books I took with me on that retreat, but I do remember and hold precious Psalm 139 and commend it to you for your journey into the presence of God.

God wants us to be present where we are.
He invites us to see and to hear what is around us and,
through it all, to discern the footprints of the Holy.
RICHARD FOSTER

THE DARK NIGHT OF THE SOUL

The Lord will guide you continually, and satisfy your needs in parched places, and make your bones strong; and you shall be like a watered garden, like a spring of water, whose waters never fail.

ISAIAH 58:11

SOMETIMES WE COME to a parched place, a spiritual desert of despair. In these times we lose all the pleasure we once experienced in our spiritual life. We long for God, but the melody in our heart is replaced with melancholy.

St. John of the Cross, a sixteenth-century monk, called these times the "dark night of the soul." In an essay by that title, he describes the work of God upon the soul, not through joy and light, but through sorrow and darkness. He writes: "God perceives the darkness within us, and because of his love for us, urges us to grow up."

As I remember from being a teenager, this is not always an easy thing to do—at least not from the standpoint of the teenager. Awkward and insecure, our lives are filled with uncomfortable firsts: first pimple, first date, first kiss, first flat tire. We are sure no one understands or appreciates what we are going through, even when we are surrounded by people who really do care and understand, people who are encouraging and supporting us all the while.

In all our awkward, lonely moments, the prophet Isaiah reminds us that we are surrounded by someone who cares: "The Lord will guide you continually, and satisfy your needs in parched places." And eventually, on the other side of our trials, we will "be like a watered garden, like a spring of water, whose waters never fail." Only then can we comfort others.

But the parched places are part of the process. Moses spent 40 years in the desert tending sheep before he had the strength and character to lead the children of Israel through the wilderness. St. Paul spent three years in the desert before he began to preach. Jesus was alone in the barren mountains of Judea for 40 days and nights before he began his ministry.

God used these dry times to give them each a source of refreshment and hope. St. John writes: "His [God's] love is not content to leave us in our weakness, and for this reason he takes us into a dark night. Through the dark night pride becomes humility, greed becomes simplicity, wrath becomes contentment, luxury becomes peace, gluttony becomes moderation, envy becomes joy, and sloth becomes strength. No soul will ever grow deep in the spiritual life unless God works passively in that soul by means of the dark night."

Lord,
I know you are there, even when I can't see you or feel your
presence. Bring me through the darkness into the light, and make
me a wellspring of joy in the lives of others.
Amen

As a deer longs for flowing streams, so my soul longs for you,
O God. My soul thirsts for God, for the living God.
When shall I come and behold the face of God? My tears have been
my food day and night, while people say to me continually,
"Where is your God?" Why are you cast down, O my soul,
And why are you disquieted within me? Hope in God;
for I shall again praise him, my help and my God.
PSALM 42:1–3, 11

WE'VE GOT THE POWER

And remember, I am with you always, to the end of the age.
MATTHEW 28:20

TECHNOLOGY IS a wonderful thing. Computers can process information faster than we can get the cap off our pen. We can connect to China via the Internet within seconds—and anywhere else in the world for that matter. The power of the electronic universe is literally at your fingertips.

But there's really nothing new about that idea. Jesus shared a similar thought with his disciples moments before his last launch into heaven. He would be with them always. They could count on his power when they needed it.

The three verses of this Great Commission form an interesting triad. Starting in verse 18, Jesus announces that "all authority" belongs to him. This authority is raw spiritual power. Jesus can make things happen. This simple truth delights and dazzles Christians: You can have your megahertz and modem speeds and all the rest; Jesus has all the power we need.

Second, Jesus gives his people a job to do: Go and make disciples. They were to spread the good news across the globe. A daunting task, to be sure. How would this crew of mostly fishermen even make a splash in the worldwide religious scene? Remember: no cell phones, no laptops, no satellite TV. They had two ways to get around the world—boats and feet. Any reasonable consultant would call this impossible.

That's where Jesus' third point comes in. He would be with them. He had already taught them about his Spirit, the Counselor, who would tell them what to say, encourage them in tough times, and give them a push when they needed it. This is better than a palm-size organizer. It's a God-size vitalizer.

At this point, it's a simple equation. If all power belongs to him, and he gives that power to his people through his Spirit, then they should be able to do just about anything. Infinity divided by X is still infinity.

Historically, those fishermen did all right. Empowered by the Spirit of Jesus, they fanned out

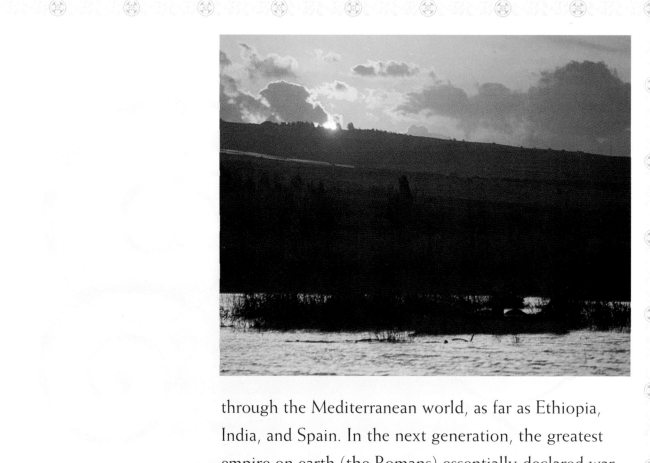

through the Mediterranean world, as far as Ethiopia, India, and Spain. In the next generation, the greatest empire on earth (the Romans) essentially declared war on Christianity, a war that lasted 250 years. Guess who won? The Christians, though their only weapon was the good news of Christ. Jesus' marching orders continued to be carried out, century after century.

When Jesus promised his presence "to the end of the age," well, that goes way past the time of his Galilean pals. The promise tumbles through the time zones to include us. We share in the task of communicating God's love in our own cultures, but we also share in this incredible power. The greatest force in the universe is with you, and his name is Jesus.

Too often we attempt to work for God to the limit of our incompetency, rather than to the limit of God's omnipotency.

HUDSON TAYLOR

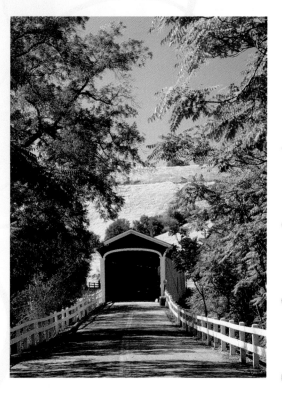

Give to the winds thy fears
Hope and be undismayed
God hears thy sighs and counts thy tears
God shall lift up thy head.

Through waves and clouds and storms,
He gently clears thy way.
Wait thou his time; so shall this night
Soon end in joyous day.

Let us in life, in death,
Thy steadfast truth declare
And publish with our latest breath
Thy love and guardian care.

PAUL GERHARDT
TRANSLATED BY JOHN WESLEY

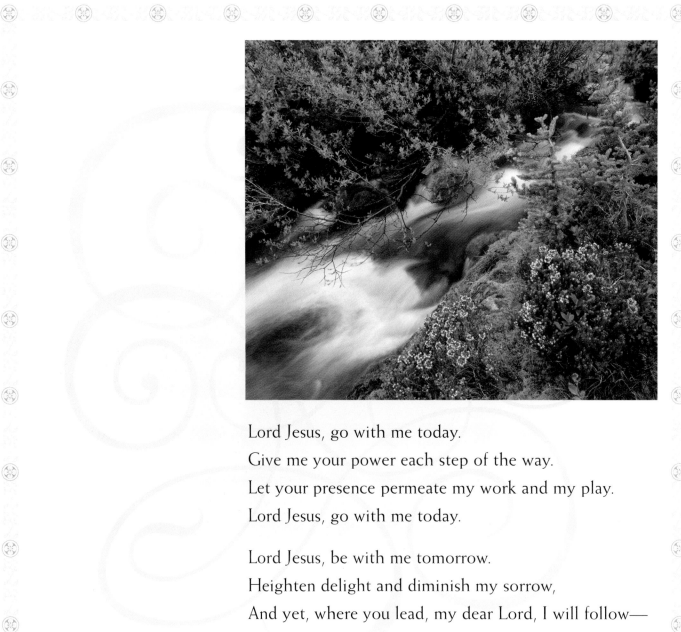

Lord Jesus, go with me today.

Give me your power each step of the way.

Let your presence permeate my work and my play.

Lord Jesus, go with me today.

Lord Jesus, be with me tomorrow.

Heighten delight and diminish my sorrow,

And yet, where you lead, my dear Lord, I will follow—

Even if some things I find hard to swallow.

Jesus, be with me tomorrow.

GATHERED IN THE PRESENCE OF GOD

For where two or three are gathered in my name,
I am there among them.

MATTHEW 18:20

I WALKED UP the winding road toward the place the bus driver pointed to in the dusk. By the time I reached the small French village at the top of the hill, it was nearly dark. There weren't any people around in the religious community of Taize, but I could hear singing. I followed the sound and pushed open the door to the building where I heard the lovely songs. I was surprised to find a candle-lit sanctuary, with hundreds of people seated on the floor around a group of monks robed in white. The beauty of the music, the dancing lights of the candles, and the feeling of peace caused me to drop to my knees and join in the worship even though I did not speak the

language. It was a holy moment, and I felt the presence of God. My weary climb up the hill was lifted into the chorus of praise and worship.

I have lived in a Quaker community where we took classes on spirituality, the arts, Quaker life and practice, and Bible study. Every morning the day would start with a half hour meeting for worship in silence. The Quakers have a word to describe a worship time in which the Holy Spirit feels present. They call such a meeting a "gathered meeting." There is a sense in which God and the people have truly "gathered," and everyone is aware of the awesomeness of the moment. I once opened my eyes to see if others felt what I was feeling or to see if there was extra light shining. I knew I was in the presence of God.

It is not only in worship services that we experience the presence of the living God. I served on a leadership team for a two-year program in spiritual formation. We would meet one week every quarter to guide the participants in their daily rituals of learning, studying, and worship. The leadership team became a place for me to experience God's presence. When we had hard decisions to make, we would trust God's work in each of us. One person sometimes had dreams that would enlighten us. Another would see many options where the others could only see one. Another made sure that we kept focusing on the impact of our decisions on the people that would be affected. We trusted each other and we trusted that God would guide us in the decisions to be made. Sometimes that took some extra time. We learned patience, and we valued each person's contribution. We were always amazed and thankful at the result. God was in our midst. We should not hesitate to ask and trust God to be present.

People gathered for genuine worship "are like a heap of fresh and burning coals warming one another as a great strength, freshness and vigor of life flows into all."
ISAAC PENINGTON

A HARVEST OF JOY

*Abide in me as I abide in you. Just as the branch
cannot bear fruit by itself unless it abides in the vine, neither can
you unless you abide in me. I am the vine, you are the branches.
Those who abide in me and I in them bear much fruit, because
apart from me you can do nothing.*

JOHN 15:4–5

ODERN-DAY management guru Stephen Covey makes much of what he calls the Law of the Farm. He says "natural consequences follow violations, in spite of good intentions." According to Covey, life operates in cycles and seasons, and the harvest is always the result of a process that involves sowing and tending and reaping.

In drawing attention to agricultural principles, Covey is following the example of Christ, who used these principles in many of his parables, including his last one. In the Upper Room, the night before the crucifixion, he talked about how his disciples could reap a rich harvest. "Bear much fruit," as he put it.

He says he is the vine, and his father is the vine dresser. We are the branches. But fruitfulness requires a process: The vine dresser will hoe out some weeds around us and cut back some of the branches. Then there is the waiting—the seasons of sunshine and rain.

As we wait we must be attached to the vine, depending on him for nourishment, support, strength, and vitality. There are so many things we can be attached to: our job, mutual fund, church, family. But to bear fruit, we have to attach ourselves to the vine.

Obviously there is no fruit from a branch that is not attached to the vine. The branch is just a channel for the life of the vine to pass through to the fruit, and as we allow his love to flow through us, we offer refreshment and joy to everyone around us.

The word Jesus uses is abide. Trust him. Obey him. Rest in him. Abide in him. Andrew Murray wrote an entire book on this parable. He says abiding in the vine is "the restful surrender of the soul to let Christ have all and work all, as completely as in nature the branch knows and seeks nothing but the vine."

So what's the promise? As we abide in him, he abides in us. This spiritual unity is reciprocal and fruitful. Jesus concludes the parable in this way: "I have said these things to you so that my joy may be in you, and that your joy may be complete" (verse 11).

That's a harvest worth waiting for.

⊛ ⊛ ⊛ ⊛

Lord,
Help me to rest in you, depending on you for all I need. And then,
Lord, please give me a harvest of joy.
Amen

⊛ ⊛ ⊛ ⊛

THE LAW OF THE FARM

According to natural laws and principles, I must prepare the ground, put in the seed, cultivate, weed and water if I expect to reap a harvest. So also in a marriage, or in helping a teenager through a difficult identity crisis—there is no quick fix, no instantaneous success formula where you can just move in by getting psyched up at some positive mental attitude rally. The law of the harvest governs. Natural laws, principles, operate regardless. So get these agricultural principles at the center of your life and your relationships. As you do your mind-set will change from a scarcity to abundance mentality.

STEPHEN COVEY, *PRINCIPLE CENTERED LEADERSHIP*

⊛ ⊛ ⊛ ⊛

IN HEAVENLY LOVE ABIDING

In heav'nly love abiding, no change my heart shall fear;
and safe is such confiding, for nothing changes here.

The storm may roar without me,
my heart may low be laid;
but God is round about me, and can
I be dismayed?
Wherever he may guide me, no
want shall turn me back;
my Shepherd is beside me, and
nothing can I lack.

His wisdom ever wakes me, his
sight is never dim;
he knows the way he takes me, and
I will walk with him.
Green pastures are before me,
which yet I have not seen;
bright skies will soon be o'er me,
where darkest clouds have been.
My hope I cannot measure, my
path to life is free;
my Savior has my treasure, and he
will walk with me.

ANNA L. WARING

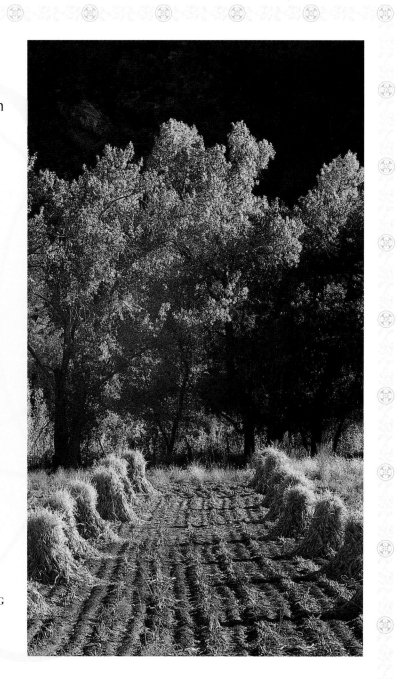

HIDE AND SEEK

And those who know your name put their trust in you, for you,
O Lord, have not forsaken those who seek you.

PSALM 9:10

EVER PLAY hide and seek as a kid? You know, where the other kids counted to 100 while you found the best secret spot, then they came hunting for you. But what if your hiding place was too good? What if they looked and looked but could not find you? Well, probably you'd help them out a little. You'd cough or sneeze to give them a clue, to keep them in the game. Or else you'd burst out of your hiding place crowing victory. Yes, the whole point is to find a good hiding place, but eventually you want to be found.

People often play hide and seek with God. It started in the Garden of Eden, when Adam and Eve sinned and then hid from God because they were ashamed. We've been playing that game ever since. There are many times when we'd prefer not to be found by him. We've got our own thing happening, and we know God will just make us feel guilty. So we pretend he's not there. We say we believe in God, but we live as if we don't.

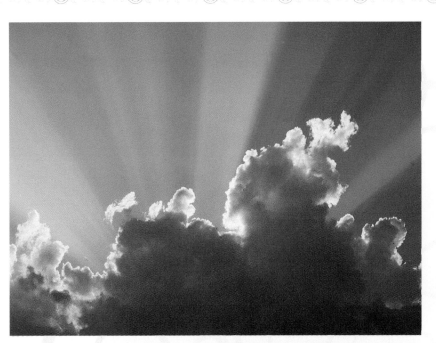

The wonderful news of the Bible is that *God seeks us.* He wants to be with us, and he'll keep hunting for us. Many Christians today are former hiders, living proof of the tenacity of God.

But sometimes it seems that God is hiding from people. The Creator can appear to be distant. When things aren't going well, we might think he doesn't care about us. When blinded by tragedy, we might fear that he's abandoned us.

But the psalmist assures us that God won't stay hidden for long. He wants us to find him. Any minute now, he'll burst out of his hiding place with a big grin. "See, I was here all along!" He does not forsake those who seek him.

Our world is full of spiritual seekers. The crass materialism of past decades has yielded a generation of folks who know there must be something more than wealth and pleasure. Today's verse is great news for these people. The living God is there for you, and he will be found, if you keep searching.

Understanding is the reward of faith. So do not seek to understand in order to believe, but believe so that you may understand.

AUGUSTINE

I've found a Friend, O such a Friend! He loved me ere I knew him.
He drew me with the cords of love, and thus he bound me to him.
And round my heart still closely twine those
ties which naught can sever,
For I am his and he is mine forever and forever.

JAMES G. SMALL

JUST A THOUGHT

One of the best things you can say to a friend is simply, "I'll be there for you." Nothing to do, nothing to prove, just the assurance of your presence when they need you. That's exactly what God tells us time and time again in the Bible. He will be there for us.

THE APPLE OF MY EYE

Guard me as the apple of the eye;
hide me in the shadow of your wings.

PSALM 17:8

WHEN MY DAUGHTER Margaret was born, I was as proud as any dad could be. It was June, and I was teaching elementary school at the time. That fall I would hold her up and proudly show her off to the parents of my new students—without even introducing my wife, who was standing right there.

Margaret was "the apple of my eye," in the way that we usually use the term. I wanted to look at her all the time. I wanted everyone to know she was mine. Now, 20 years later, I still like to look at her. I'll watch her from across a room, talking with strangers or playing with children or reading a book. She has grown into a lovely young woman, and I think I may be just as proud of her now as I was then, although not nearly as possessive.

That's because the way I see her has changed, as has my understanding of the phrase "apple of my eye." I

used to think it merely meant pride, like a farmer show-ing off a good crop or a dad holding out his child for all the world to see. But the Hebrew term translated five times in the Authorized Version of the Bible as "apple of the eye" has nothing to do with fruit.

It actually means "little man," referring to the image we see if we look closely into the eyes of someone else. Another meaning is "daughter," in perhaps the same sense. The Hebrews meant it as the pupil of the eye, a place where we can see a reflection of ourselves and through which we see the things we love. Of course that's what I see when I see Margaret now, a kinder and—thankfully—prettier version of myself. I still brag on her a little and embarrass her a lot. That's because who she is reflects well on me and on the contributions I've made in her life.

It's comforting to think of God seeing us that way— as the apple of his eye, a reflection of himself. We bear his image; we are his sons and daughters. So he looks on us with pride and holds us up for the angels to see. "Look, this is my child, the apple of my eye."

It's no wonder he guards us, not just as his children but as the pupil of his own eye. We have many reflexes that serve to protect our eyes. They are sensitive and precious, and we guard them carefully. Our eyes are important because we use them to see what we love.

And so does he.

Lord,
Thank you for making me in your own image. See me as you see
yourself, and love me as you love your own Son. Help me to be
more like you, and guard me as the apple of your eye.
Amen.

UNDER HIS WINGS

Under his wings I am safely abiding,
though the night deepens and tempests are wild;
still I can trust him, I know he will keep me,
he has redeemed me and I am his child.

Under his wings, what a refuge in sorrow!
How the heart yearningly turns to his rest!
Often when earth has no balm for my healing,
there I find comfort and there I am blest.

Under his wings, O what precious enjoyment!
There will I hide till life's trials are o'er;

sheltered, protected, no evil can harm me,
resting in Jesus I'm safe evermore.

Under his wings, under his wings,
who from his love can sever?
Under his wings my soul shall abide,
safely abide forever.

WILLIAM O. CUSHING

GOD PROMISES HIS LOVE

✤ ✤ ✤ ✤

HOW PRECIOUS is your steadfast love, O God! All people may take refuge in the shadow of your wings.

PSALM 36:7

TASTING STEADFAST LOVE

*But I trusted in your steadfast love; my heart shall
rejoice in your salvation. I will sing to the Lord,
because he has dealt bountifully with me.*

PSALM 13:5–6

STEADFAST LOVE is a love that lasts, a love that is constant and enduring. You can count on this kind of love. Have you experienced this kind of love or at least a taste of it? It is a love that tells you something about God.

Parents can show some of this steadfast love. I grew a beard and long hair as soon as I went away to college. I was at a fine Christian college and my parents had some images of what a fine Christian student should look like. They were surprised, actually shocked, when they saw me. It would not be the only time I made a choice that surprised or disappointed them, but they never ceased to love me. They were steadfast in their loving concern, while at the same time giving me freedom to make my own choices.

Longtime friends and loving spouses can also give us clues to this steadfast love. A friend who keeps contact

even though the distance is great testifies to an enduring love. Letters, phone calls, even e-mail have become
the avenues of support and care. A spouse who knows
our moods, who recognizes our shortcomings, and who
still loves us is a sign of this steadfast love.

These testimonies of human love are clues to the
amazing love of God. Psalm 13 begins as a lament, asking where God is in the midst of pain and sorrow, asking how long enemies will seem to get the upper hand.
The poet's concerns are poured out to God, but there is
no doubt about the final outcome. God's love is sure.

I rely on your constant love; I will be glad because you will rescue me. I will sing to you, O Lord, because you have been good to me.

PSALM 13:6, TEV

God's salvation is promised. God will act and give reason to sing.

When we see signs of God's love, when we feel like singing, we are entering a world of gratitude. Our lives become so aware of God's love that we find ourselves being filled with thanksgiving. We remember and respond to God's steadfast love with gratitude. In my journal, I keep a gratitude list. Each day during my prayer time, I jot down one thing I have noticed that I am thankful for. I give God thanks for the birds I hear singing, the roses in Mrs. Cain's yard, the good game my son played in baseball. The person who suggested that I keep a list said I should try not to repeat anything, that way I will sharpen my perceptions and look beyond the obvious. So I have thanked God for the smell of spring, the joke my daughter told, a long nap. It pushes me to see God's love at work in all the circumstances of life. We have even started to keep a gratitude journal in our house so all family members can add a prayer or note of thanksgiving.

Another response to the steadfast love of God is praise: "I will sing." I am not the greatest singer, but I know the value of singing songs of praise. To praise

God in song lifts me to a joyous frame of mind. Forgotten are the lists and tasks still to accomplish. I am caught up in something larger than myself. I feel my whole self involved, my voice, the deepening of breath, the warmth of my body using energy to create music. I turn my focus from my particular needs to recognizing the God who is loving me and who is working for good in my world.

This is a good day to look back at all the ways God's love has been present in your life. You may wish to write a prayer of thanks, start a gratitude journal, or sing a song of praise. God has and will continue to love you and deal bountifully with you!

A slowness to applaud betrays a cold temper or an envious spirit.

HANNAH MORE

ICE CREAM MEMORIES

*Do not remember the sins of my youth or my transgressions;
according to your steadfast love remember me, for your
goodness' sake, O Lord!*

PSALM 25:7

ED WAS SEVEN YEARS OLD, scuffling with Joe, his six-year-old cousin, over an ice cream cone. Ed reached for the cone, Joe swung it out of his grasp, and the dollop of ice cream soared across the room, splatting against the front door. At that moment Uncle Bob appeared, saw the melting glob on the door, and scolded both boys. Ed felt terrible.

Oh, the sins of youth! Many of us remember misdeeds far more serious than this. Big or small, they find their way into our deepest memories and fester there.

As Ed grew up, he often recalled the ice cream incident and always felt bad about it. Years later, just before Joe's wedding, Ed brought it up again. "Hey, this may sound silly, but I still feel bad about grabbing for your ice cream cone when we were kids. I was wrong, and I'm still sorry about it."

"What are you talking about?" Joe said.

Ed described the scene again, but Joe had completely forgotten it. The sin that had plagued Ed for
nearly two decades was not remembered by the one he
had sinned against. He felt as if a weight had been lifted
from his shoulders.

That's the psalmist's prayer—that God would
remember him but completely forget the sins of his
youth. We can make the same request. All those regrets
we have about people we hurt, errors we made, or roads
we did not take—we can bring these before our loving
Lord. As we confess these sins, he lifts the burden off
our shoulders. As he said through Jeremiah: "I will for-

give their iniquity, and remember their sin no more" (Jeremiah 31:34).

How does this work? Is God's memory faulty? Does he have trouble recalling things—as so many of us do as the years go by? Not at all. It's just that he chooses to forget the sins he has forgiven. He decides not to think about them. The debt has been paid. They don't matter anymore.

But he remembers us—vividly. We are members of his family, and he delights in thinking about us.

In the witty musical *The Fantasticks*, the veteran actor Henry bumbles about, misquotes lines, and generally makes a mess of things. He keeps crowing about his past successes, the glory days when the spotlight never left him, but it's obvious now his best days are behind him. As he makes his final exit, he pleads, "Remember me . . . in light." That's exactly how God remembers us—not in the messes we so regularly make for ourselves, but in the dazzling light of his love.

Since nothing we intend is ever faultless, and nothing
we attempt ever without error, and nothing we achieve
without some measure of finitude and fallibility we call
humanness, we are saved by forgiveness.

DAVID AUGSBURGER, *CARING ENOUGH TO FORGIVE*

Remember me, O Lord, but let's

Ignore my adolescent crimes.

Remember me, but please forget

The errors of my earlier times.

The blood of Christ can cover up

My callow deeds of waste and want.

I trust you, Lord, to overlook

The wrongs I've done that haze and haunt

My days and nights. Forgive my sin,

Turn wrong to right, and teach my soul

Your easy peace. Enfold me in

Your awesome love, and take control.

Forget my sins, but when you see

Me praying, Lord, remember *me*.

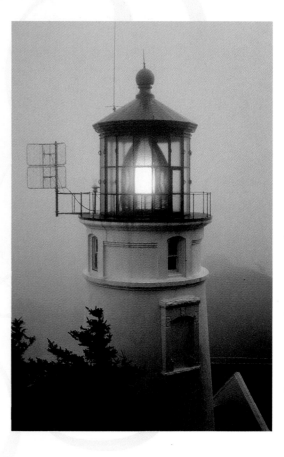

Love That Lasts

Let your steadfast love, O Lord, be upon us, even as we hope in you.
Psalm 33:22

My wife and I have been married 25 years—quite an accomplishment these days.

The first few years were pretty rough, however. She had come from an abusive home, the seventh of ten kids. She had trouble believing I loved her; in fact, she had trouble believing anybody did. Fortunately, both of us understood from the beginning that marriage wasn't just about being in love—it was about choosing to love. Because of that, we have managed to survive some pretty tough times together.

The first ten years were the hardest. I was working two jobs. She was alone with the kids. We would go days without talking, lying in bed at night silent and angry and frustrated. Her short temper was matched by my stubborn silence. Finally, by God's grace, we became friends and lovers again.

Our experience was nothing like that of the prophet Hosea, however. At God's command, he loved and mar-

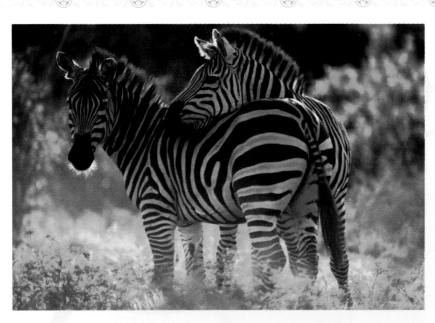

ried a harlot named Gomer. At first she loved him and even bore him a son, though she never quite gave up her loose ways. We can imagine that while he was out preaching, she was out partying—her makeup a little too heavy and her laughter a little too loud. Hosea wasn't even sure he was the father of their next two children. Gomer eventually left Hosea and returned to a life of prostitution. He finally locked her out of the house.

But God told Hosea to find her and bring her home. So Hosea did. In fact, he even had to buy her back from her pimp.

He didn't just take her back, however. He loved her. And in doing so, he made more converts than he ever could have by preaching. It was a practical demonstration of *hesed*, the Hebrew word for a steadfast, loyal, faithful love.

This is the word the psalmist uses three times in Psalm 33. It is a love that lasts, because "the counsel of the Lord stands forever, the thoughts of his heart to all generations" (verse 11). This constant, purposeful love is the kind of love that makes a relationship work, whether the relationship is between a man and woman, a parent and child, or God and his people.

It's the kind of love that gives us hope.

⊛   ⊛   ⊛   ⊛

Lord,
You love me with a faithful love, even when I am unfaithful.
May your patience and forgiveness give me confidence and joy,
and may I love others as you have loved me.
Amen.

⊛   ⊛   ⊛   ⊛

IMMORTAL LOVE, FOREVER FULL

Immortal love, forever full

forever flowing free,

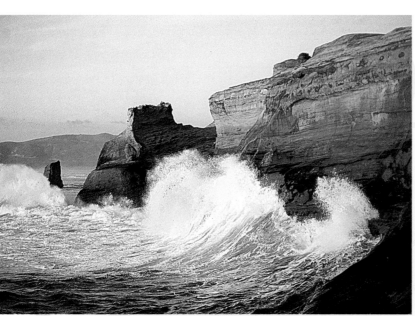

forever shared, forever whole,
a never ebbing sea.

Through him the first fond prayers are said,
our lips of childhood frame;
the last low whispers of our dead
are burdened by his name.

O Lord and master of us all,
whate'er our name or sign,
we own thy sway, we hear thy call
we test our lives by thine.

JOHN GREENLEAF WHITTIER

GOD KNOWS OUR MIDDLE NAMES

Do not fear, for I have redeemed you;
I have called you by name, you are mine.

ISAIAH 43:1

MANY PEOPLE do not use their middle names. They have seldom heard them used except perhaps when Mom or Dad were really angry—and the whole name, middle and all, were called out. So a lot of us may not even have positive feelings about our middle name, hearing it used only when we were in trouble. Others of us have been saddled with middle names we would rather forget. We were named after a dead uncle or an eccentric aunt. The name may have been popular at one time, but now it is not. We may use a middle initial when we have to write our legal name, but often our middle name remains hidden on some faraway birth certificate.

I have never used my middle name. It isn't that I don't like it, rather it makes my name too long and cumbersome. I seldom heard my middle name until I went to England and one of my close colleagues took to calling me "James." The English twang was so delightful that even though "James" sounded like some classy butler or chauffeur, I gained a new appreciation for my middle name.

I liked the sound of it, and I heard echoes of the words of Isaiah, "I have called you by name, you are mine."

Some years later I was on a retreat in the wilderness of British Columbia. During a time of prayer, I had some incredible dialogues with Jesus. I did not see him or hear him, but I felt his presence and heard him say to me, "I want you to be James."

Strangely enough, I had never associated my middle name with any of the people named James in the Bible. When Jesus invited me to be James, I wasn't too keen on the idea. Wasn't James one of the "sons of thunder" (along with his brother John) who was called to be a disciple of Jesus and at one point wanted to get the best seat in the new Kingdom of God (Mark 10:35–45)? Wasn't there another James who was a leader making rules for the new church in Jerusalem while Peter and Paul were out in the mission field converting the gentiles and building the New Testament church? I wasn't sure I liked the idea of being an "old James," more concerned about keeping order than in creating new ministries. In

response to my questions, Jesus reminded me that it was important to hold the center even as others push the edges. And, "do not fear, for I have redeemed you; I have called you by name, you are mine."

Whatever fears I have about the unfolding of that prayer dialogue are met by an overwhelming sense of being named and loved. God knows my middle name. God loves me and calls me by name. God has work for me to do, but first I must discover a God who loves me, claims me, and knows me by name.

To call somebody by name is to be in a relationship. In the beginning of Genesis, God gave man and woman the power to name the animals and plants and the world of creation around them. Thus we have a relationship with the birds and animals, the flowing rivers, and the towering mountains. But even before our relationship to creation was established, we had a relationship with God—who called us by name and also claimed us as beloved sons and daughters. The words of Isaiah take root and flower in great beauty and strength inside us. We are not to be afraid. We are called by name. We are loved by God. We belong.

I am still growing into claiming my middle name. I am still learning what it means to "hold the center as others push the edges." But I have a wonderful sense of God's love, and I know God calls each of us by name and promises to hold us in love.

*Loving God,
I place all my names before you. Let me hear your voice calling me. Let me know your embrace loving me. Let me feel your power strengthening me. Let me experience your calm chasing away my fears. Loving God, I open myself to your love. Amen.*

LARRY J. PEACOCK, *WATER WORDS*

THERE'S NO PLACE FOR HOME

As the Father has loved me, so I have loved you; abide in my love.
If you keep my commandments, you will abide in my love, just as
I have kept my Father's commandments and abide in his love.

JOHN 15:9–10

MICHELLE HAS A PROBLEM: She has no home. She's not homeless exactly. You might say she has too many homes. When she went to college, her parents lived in New Jersey. That's where she grew up. But her parents just moved to Michigan, and that has thrown her emotions into turmoil.

"I don't have a *place* anymore, a place that's really mine," she complains. Oh, the college dorm is all right, but it's not really a home, just a parking lot with beds and computers. Michelle has friends in New Jersey, and she could stay at a number of houses there, but that's not her home anymore, either. She visits her parents on school vacations, but their new house is strange to her, and she has to bunk with her little sister. Michelle still has to help with the dishes, but she has to ask which cupboards they belong in. It's not her home.

Certainly there are worse problems to have. The poor who sleep in city parks won't have much sympathy for a young woman with three different places to live—or maybe they would. It's important to have a home, a place that's yours, somewhere you can abide.

That's the word Jesus used with his disciples in his farewell discourse at the Last Supper. Abide in my love. Sit down, kick your feet up, stay a while. Make yourself at home. The offer also extends to modern-day disciples. We can have a place in the heart of God. We can make our home there.

A home helps to make you who you are. Your family instills certain values and habits, and your neighborhood teaches you certain ways, too. We find distinct qualities in people from, say, New York or L.A., from the farm or the suburbs, from the Midwest or the deep South. We also see that children resemble their parents, not only in looks but in mannerisms, interests, and careers. Our homes mold us.

So when we find our spiritual home in the love of God, what does that mean? It means our lives are shaped by that love. We take comfort in God's love and we share it with others. And, as Jesus says in these verses, we need to "keep his commandments." Not to earn God's love—that would be bribery—but as a loving response to the undeserved love we receive from God.

There are always house rules, in a college dorm or a suburban split-level, whether it's "No lacrosse in the halls" or "You take out the trash, I feed the dog." But the people who feel most at home don't mind the rules. Those rules are simply the way that a home functions

O Lord,
Be my home. Let me rest in you,
live in you, come home to you.
I want to abide in your love.
Write your commandments on
my heart so my greatest desire
is to honor you with my life.
As I work and play, as I talk
and pray, surround all my
doings with your energizing
presence.
In your holy name,
Amen.

best. It's the same way with God's love. For those who abide there, keeping the commandments comes naturally. Surrounded by love, we act with love.

ABIDE WITH ME

Abide with me, fast falls the eventide;
The darkness deepens; Lord, with me abide!
When other helpers fail and comforts flee,
Help of the helpless, O abide with me.

I need thy presence every passing hour;
What but thy grace can foil the tempter's power?
Who like thyself, my guide and stay can be?
Through cloud and sunshine, Lord, abide with me.

HENRY F. LYTE

To be with God, there is no need to be continually in
church. We may make [a chapel] of our heart
wherein to retire from time to time to converse with
him in meekness, humility, and love. There is not in
the world a kind of life more sweet and delightful
than that of a continual conversation with God.

BROTHER LAWRENCE

A NEW IDENTITY

I give you a new commandment, that you love one another.
Just as I have loved you, you also should love one another.
By this everyone will know you are my disciples,
if you have love for one another.

JOHN 13:34–35

IT HAD BEEN a hard week. Together with his disciples, Jesus had made the long trip from Galilee to Jerusalem, about 100 miles. Before arriving in the city, they had spent the night in Jericho at the home of a tax collector named Zacchaeus. They then hiked up the steep, rocky hills to Bethany, where Jesus usually stayed with his friends Martha and Mary.

The roads were crowded; there were many pilgrims gathering for the Passover. On Sunday, many of them had gathered around him, escorting him on a donkey to the temple. "Hosanna," they cried, laying palm branches in the street before him. Each day that week he went to the temple to teach; he also healed the sick and drove the money changers out of the courtyard.

The demands on him were many, and political intrigue swirled around the young Jewish rabbi. His teachings were challenged daily by the priests, as the people pressed around him, clamoring for a king. Thursday was especially hectic. It was the first day of the Feast of Unleavened Bread, and the temple was a frenzy of activity as the Passover lambs—as many as 200,000 of them—were slain.

It's not hard to imagine the need he must have felt to withdraw to a quiet upstairs apartment on Mount Zion and have a meal with his closest friends. It was there, as they shared bread and wine, that he transformed an ancient Jewish ritual into the Lord's Supper, the cornerstone of the Christian liturgy.

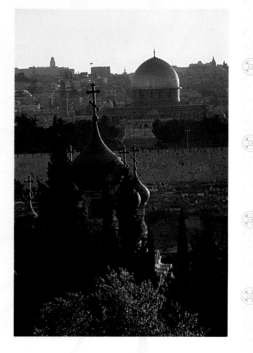

But this event was more than a meal. There were lessons to be learned and good-byes to be said. He began by washing the disciples' feet, dusty from the crowded city streets. This was the job of a servant, and it was a role he expected them to take. "I have set you an example, that you should do as I have done to you," he said (John 13:15).

And after Judas slipped out into the dark night to betray him, Jesus began to talk with his disciples about his death and about their future. It would be a long weekend for them all, filled with despair, and he encouraged them with many promises.

He promised to prepare a place for them in his Father's house. He promised to send the Holy Spirit to guide them. He promised to return. And then he prayed a long, poignant prayer for their safety and unity and joy.

This discourse in the Upper Room reveals more about Jesus' heart than any other passage of Scripture. It was in this context that he said, "I give you a new commandment, that you love one another. Just as I have loved you, you also should love one another. By this everyone will know you are my disciples, if you have love for one another."

At first glance this seems like a simple command: Love one another. And it is, of course, the foundation of all his ethical teaching. But if we look more closely, we see it is a promise, too. He offered his followers— and us—a new identity. If we keep the command, others will know that we are his disciples. It's a simple but profound promise: If we love each other, people will know we love him.

This is what one theologian called "the mark of a Christian." We are not asked to love everyone in some broad, general way, although that is a good thing. But

BLEST FEAST OF LOVE DIVINE
Blest feast of love divine!
'Tis grace that makes
    us free
to feed upon this bread
    and wine,
in memory Lord of thee.

That blood which flowed
    for sin,
in symbol here we see,
and feel the blessed
    pledge within
that we are loved
    by thee.

SIR EDWARD DENNY

we are asked to love each other in very tangible, specific ways. We are to wash each others' feet, so to speak. We are to make sacrifices.

The next day Jesus would show what this meant, laying his life down for us all. Every day we can do the same thing by giving a smile or a hug in his name, by stooping to encourage a small child, by offering a cup of cold water to a stranger, by going out of our way to keep a promise.

Of course, some of us will make sacrifices that are more costly. We may sit and comfort a dying loved one for weeks on end or give many dollars or hours to a worthy cause. But whenever we do these things we show others both what we love—and who we love.

It's a promise.

Dear God,
Help me to love others as you
have loved me. Thank you for
the privilege of being like your
son as I love and serve those
around me.
Amen.

The height to which love exalts is unspeakable. Love unites us to God. Love covers a multitude of sins. Love beareth all things, is long-suffering in all things. There is nothing base, nothing arrogant in love. By love have all the elect of God been made perfect.

CLEMENT OF ROME

TURNING TO GOD'S LOVE

They who have my commandments and keep them are those who love me; and those who love me will be loved by my Father, and I will love them and reveal myself to them.

JOHN 14:21

SOMEONE ONCE WROTE, "God loves both more than you and before you." Love is the defining characteristic of God. God's love is first, primary. We cannot get up early and beat God to loving. There is no place we can travel and not find God's love already present. God's very nature is love.

Douglas Steere, a wonderful Quaker teacher and writer, liked to say that God is forever wooing us and besieging us with love. It is a startling image to imagine that God is wooing us like a lover, passionately seeking us and yearning for our response. Not only is the nature of God love, but the activity of God is love and the focus of that wooing love is us. God wants us to respond to the courting. We will not find our true home until we turn and respond to the love of God.

The Bible is full of stories of God's love. It begins with creation; God created a world of beauty to call our attention to the Master Designer. God created humans with love, forming them in his own image and filling them with his own breath. We were kissed into being, given eyes to see the wonders of creation and hearts to know that we are connected to the heart of God.

When we turned away, forgot our Maker, and became captives in Egypt, God sent Moses to lead us to freedom and remind us of the great love of God. The story of the Exodus from Egypt has continued to be a shaping story that tells us of the great love of God. Many of the psalms are songs telling that story of redemption. "He [the Lord] made known his ways to Moses, his acts to the people of Israel. The Lord is merciful and gracious, slow to anger and abounding in steadfast love" (Psalm 103:7–8).

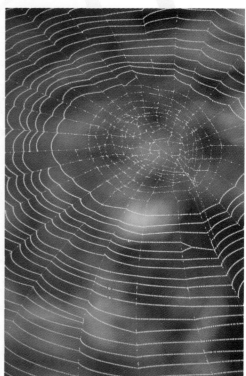

In the New Testament, we meet Jesus, who is the clearest picture of God's love. God was willing to send his Son that we might see how great God's love is. The wooing of God is personal, and we get an incredible picture of God's love by the stories that Jesus told. Perhaps no story gives a better picture than the parable of the waiting father and prodigal son.

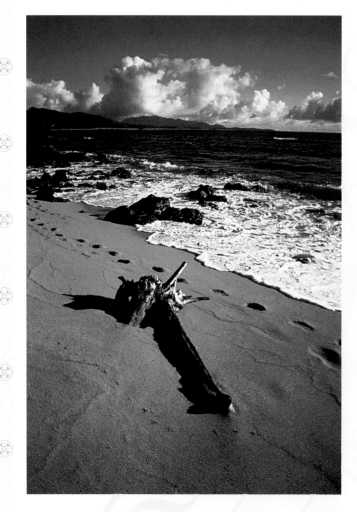

Though the son wanders off to spend his inheritance, still the father longs for the son. The father runs to greet the wayward child on his return. The welcome becomes a party and the relationship of child to parent is strengthened and deepened (Luke 15:11–32).

In our verse from John 14, the meeting between God and humanity has occurred. The followers of Jesus have experienced the besieging love of God and have turned toward it. As they enter into that love, they are given instructions on how to deepen the relationship. The instructions are Jesus' commandments to "Love your God with all your heart, and with all your soul, and with all your mind, and with all your strength" and "You shall love your neighbor as yourself" (Mark 12:30–31). Jesus says that those who live these commandments will find themselves in constant communion with God, and more of the love of God will be revealed to them. That is a promise.

IDENTITY CRISIS

See what love the Father has given us, that we should be called children of God; and that is what we are.

1 JOHN 3:1

OHN AND JOSIE have a daughter, Karin. They waited a long time to be parents, and it's obvious they're enjoying it. Their whole church enjoys watching this family, and it's delightful to see little Karin resemble her parents more and more as she grows.

It's not unusual to see a child take after his or her parents. We often comment on children being "a chip off the old block," or a "spittin' image" of a parent. As we pass DNA from one generation to the next, certain physical characteristics are shared. You get your dad's big nose, your mom's gentle eyes, maybe your grandpa's potbelly. Interests are also shared, often careers. Phone books are full of businesses that have the ending "& Son," and in another generation we'll have some businesses with the "& Daughter" ending. Kids go fishing with their folks or attend the theater, establishing habits they'll carry throughout their lives. We are our parents'

progeny, and that determines a great deal of who we turn out to be.

The thing about John and Josie, though, is that they adopted little Karin when she was already 1½. Karin doesn't have their DNA, but amazingly she still resembles her adoptive parents, and more so every week.

And that's a picture of our relationship with God. He has adopted us into his family, and now we're his children. As we spend more and more time with him, we become more and more like him. We share his interests, his values, his characteristics. We go into his line of work, helping people, being creative, finding others to adopt.

Love makes this happen. God's astounding love reaches out for us when we have nothing to offer. He makes us his own children and pours his love into our hearts. His love transforms us, giving us a new identity.

We live in a time when people are desperately trying to "find themselves." Major magazines run tests where you check off certain answers and the tests give you adjectives to describe your personality. "If you scored 50 to 100, you're polite and easygoing. If 25 to 49, you're mean and surly." Bookstores are crammed with volumes on self-awareness. We have colors, seasons, planets, temperaments, and scads of initials to label ourselves. But still we cry, *"Who am I?"*

John puts it so simply in 1 John 3:1. As we accept God's love, we can call ourselves the children of God. "And that is what we are." We are adopted through the sacrifice of Jesus into a new family. We have a new name, a new nature.

In Romans 8, the Apostle Paul discusses this new life we have. We are to live by God's Spirit, rejecting our old, selfish desires. But no longer are we enslaved to fear. We don't behave ourselves because we're afraid of the consequences of misbehaving. Not anymore. We have received "the spirit of adoption." We're not slaves in the household of faith, but beloved children. We strive to please God with our lives because that is who we are. The Spirit is constantly whispering to our hearts that we are, indeed, God's own (Romans 8:15–16).

So rest in that assurance. When you're not sure who you are or how much you matter, listen to those divine whispers. God loves you dearly, as his own child. And that is what you are.

Love divine, all loves excelling,
joy of heav'n to earth come down,
fix in us thy humble dwelling,
all thy faithful mercies crown.
Jesus, thou art all compassion,
pure, unbounded love thou art;
visit us with thy salvation,
enter ev'ry trembling heart.

Breathe, O breathe thy loving Spirit
into ev'ry troubled breast;
let us all in thee inherit,
let us find thy promised rest.

take away our bent to sinning,
Alpha and Omega be;
end of faith, as its beginning,
set our hearts at liberty.

Finish then thy new creation,
pure and spotless let us be;
let us see thy great salvation,
perfectly restored in thee.
Changed from glory into glory,
till in heav'n we take our place,
till we cast our crowns before thee,
lost in wonder, love, and praise!

CHARLES WESLEY

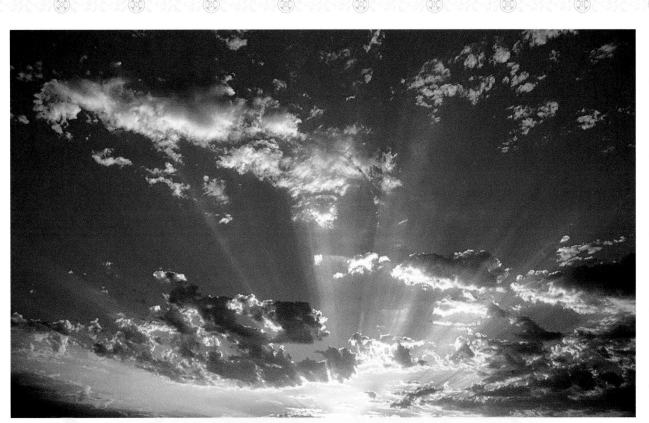

Lord,
Let me bask in your awesome love. Let me rest in your presence.
I've been away, like the prodigal son, wasting my life
in selfish pursuits.
But now I'm back, longing to be wrapped in your warm arms.
Forgive me, I pray, welcome me back again.
Let me see the dazzling light of your smile, as we dine together.
Teach me your wisdom, show me your way,
share with me your wants.
Remind me again of who I am—and whose I am.
In devoted love,
Amen.

WHY GOD SHOULD BE LOVED

Beloved, let us love one another, because love is from God; everyone who loves is born of God and knows God. Whoever does not love does not know God, for God is love.

1 JOHN 4:7–8

OUTSIDE OF the Apostle John, perhaps no man ever thought so deeply and wrote more passionately about the love of God than St. Bernard of Clairvaux. He wrote 66 sermons on the first two chapters of the Song of Solomon alone, and his writings influenced many Christian thinkers.

The son of a noble French family, Bernard became a monk at the age of 22. Just three years later he was sent to establish a new monastery in Clairvaux, the Valley of Light. The beginnings of this small community of faith were difficult. Their bread was the coarsest of barley, and sometimes boiled beech leaves served as vegetables. The monks went short of even the bare necessities, and Bernard himself fell ill.

The 12 monks under his charge were disillusioned at the severity of their lives together, and Bernard reconsidered his responsibilities to the community under his charge. He tempered his demands and wrote a Charter of Charity for his order. He began to take seriously the love of God and how it affects us.

His famous essay "On the Love of God" gives us some insight into the heart of this man who many consider the last of the Church Fathers. He begins by answering the question: "Why should God be loved?" The answer is that he deserves to be loved. "I find no other worthy reason for loving him except himself," he says.

But according to Bernard, that's not how we start. At first we love ourselves for our own sake. Fortunately, this love of self is held in check by the command to love our neighbor—and to do this we must see that God is the cause of our love. "You cannot love your neighbor if you do not love God," he says.

We can also love God for our own sake—because he can meet our needs. "When we suffer some calamity, some storm in our lives, we turn to God and ask for help," Bernard observes. But he does not think this is a bad thing: "This is how we who love ourselves begin to love God."

Whoever does not love does not know God, for God is love.
I JOHN 4:8

Help me love you for yourself, and love others as you love me. Change me as you love me, and help me taste the sweetness of your grace. Amen.

But there is a better, higher kind of love, a love of God for God's sake. This should be the plane to which we should all aspire. It comes as we are softened by our experiences, and in our constant prayers we "taste" the grace of God. Bernard writes: "Once God's sweetness has been tasted, it draws us to the pure love of God more than our needs compel us to love him."

This understanding will transform us. "When we begin to feel this, it will not be hard to fulfill the commandment to love our neighbor. We love because we are loved. We care for others because Jesus cares for us."

Bernard would test this notion in his own life. A popular preacher, he became embroiled in papal politics, often acting as an emissary to settle disputes. Late in life, at the request of the pope, he recruited an army for an unpopular and unsuccessful Crusade. It failed because of infighting, but he was a peacemaker until the end, leaving his sick bed to settle a dispute between the citizens of Metz and the Duke of Lorraine.

His life itself confirmed the promise of the Apostle John in his first letter to the churches. God's love transforms us, enabling us to love. If we love God, we will love each other.

JESUS, THOU JOY OF LOVING HEARTS

Jesus, thou joy of loving hearts,
thou fount of life, thou light of men,
from the poor bliss that earth imparts,
we turn unfilled to thee again.

Thy truth unchanged has ever stood;
thou savest those who on thee call
to them that seek thee, thou art good,
to them that find thee, all in all.

We taste thee, O thou living Bread,
and long to feast upon thee still;

we drink of thee, the fountainhead,
and thirst our souls from thee to fill.

Our restless spirits yearn for thee,
where're our changeful lot is cast
glad, when thy gracious smile we see,
blest when our faith can hold thee fast.

O Jesus with us ever stay;
make all our moments calm and bright,
chase the dark night of sin away;
shed over the world thy holy light.

ST. BERNARD OF CLAIRVAUX

GOD PROMISES JOY AND PEACE

AY THE GOD of hope
fill you with all joy and
peace in believing, so
that you may abound in
hope by the power of the Holy Spirit.

ROMANS 15:13

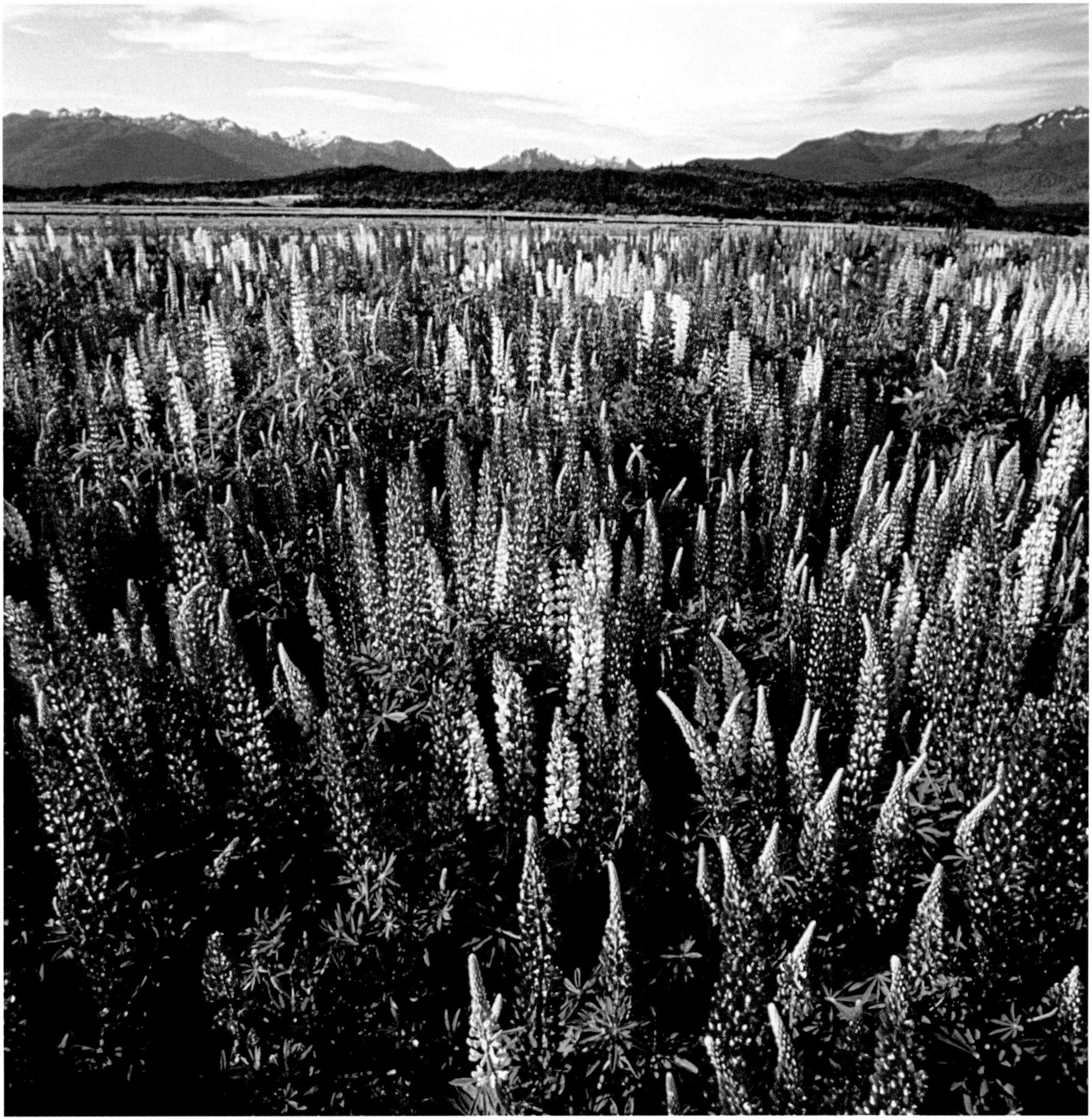

THE ANGEL OF PEACE

*Peace I leave with you; my peace I give to you.
I do not give to you as the world gives. Do not let
your hearts be troubled, and do not let them be afraid.*

JOHN 14:27

THESE WORDS OF JESUS are some of the most comforting in the Bible. Jesus brings us God's peace. It is a different peace than the world gives. It is a deep and lasting peace, no matter what troubles are going on around you. I read these words and feel a great wave of calm wash over me. I am thankful to be in the presence of God—who brings inner peace and outward hope, who settles the troubled heart and dissolves our fears.

The world most often talks about peace as the absence of war. In many countries where there is still fighting and bloodshed, where war still works its destruction, this is a peace that is desired and necessary. It is right to pray and work for an end to killing in these places of violence. It is hard to have any kind of peace as long as people experience the destruction of their lives and property.

Yet the absence of war does not insure that there is peace. There can still be hunger, poverty, resentment, bitterness, and distrust that get in the way of living together in peace. Many nations have found building peace and reconciliation as hard as stopping the fighting. One of the first things the new government in South Africa did after the system of discrimination known as apartheid was dismantled was to appoint a minister of reconciliation. The new president knew that the anger and resentments from the past needed to be addressed, so he chose a well-respected bishop to lead the efforts of reconciliation.

The peace that Jesus leaves is deeper than national policy or the absence of war. Jesus brings a peace that not only encompasses the absence of war but takes up residence inside us. God's peace is an inside job. God's peace is forgiveness for our past mistakes and courage for the future. God's peace keeps our hearts untroubled and unafraid. God's peace gives us a perspective to encounter the world and its violence with a calm and enduring presence. God's peace is the knowledge that we do not face the world alone. We are accompanied by God, within us and all around us.

In our sanctuary there is a small ceramic angel that sits on our communion table. It just showed up after we'd had a number of funerals in the congregation, including a four-year-old boy who drowned and a 23-year-old man who died of a drug overdose. These deaths deeply affected the community, and in the midst of the grief there were also doubts, questions, and anger. How could God let this happen to ones so young and full of life? Where was God? That's when the angel appeared. I don't know who brought it and left it for us, but I like the sense that, in the midst of our grieving, God sent an angel to remind us where to take our questions and who it is that brings us peace. The angel silently sits there as a testimony to the mysterious yet comforting presence of God. In the midst of sorrow we seek a deeper peace that will not only get us through the days but give us the courage to live joyfully, thankfully, and unafraid.

The Hebrew word for peace is *shalom*. The word carries a sense of inner peace and the sense of well-being in the community. It is not only a greeting for individuals, but it also describes the nature of life lived within a community. The Jewish understanding can broaden our understanding of peace to move beyond the individual to incorporate the wider community.

The peace God gives passes all understanding, yet it is experienced by you and me. Celebrate the peace given to us: Shalom!

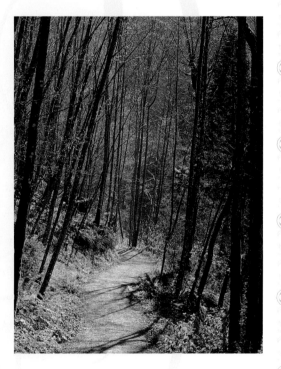

LIKE A RIVER GLORIOUS

Like a river glorious is God's perfect peace,
over all victorious in its bright increase;
perfect, yet it floweth fuller every day,
perfect, yet it groweth deeper all the way.

Ev'ry joy or trial falleth from above,
traced upon our dial by the sun of love;
we may trust him fuller all for us to do—
they who trust him wholly find him wholly true.

Stayed upon Jehovah, hearts are fully blest—
finding, as he promised, perfect peace and rest.

FRANCES RIDLEY HAVERGAL

JOY

*I have said these things to you so that my joy may
be in you, and that your joy may be complete.*

JOHN 15:11

IKE HAD GREAT NEWS. He had been accepted at the city's college for the performing arts. Now he needed a scholarship so he could afford to go there, but the chances of this looked pretty good. It seemed that he was on his way to a bright new future, in which he could use his considerable acting talent. It was a joyous day.

The following weeks piled joy on top of joy. He did get the scholarship and was able to enroll. He started classes a few months later. The curriculum was tough, but Mike worked hard. The students were a bit snobbish at first, but Mike's gentle spirit soon won them over. Recently he appeared in a school musical—a small role, but he performed well. Joy on top of joy on top of joy.

Good news often comes to us like this, in pieces. We rejoice over one thing that promises better things. Joy often rides a rough road—hard work, some setbacks—but it's worth the trip.

*With an eye made quiet
by the power of harmony,
and the deep power of joy,
we see into the life of things.*
WILLIAM WORDSWORTH

Jesus had already brought great joy to his disciples. By calling them to follow him, he welcomed them on a wild adventure. They had front-row seats for his teaching, his healings, his squabbles with the religious leaders. They went through storms with Jesus, hungry days and sleepless nights, but they were *living*, perhaps for the first time in their lives. He had announced that his purpose was to give his people life—more than that: *abundant* life, life overflowing. That's what they were already enjoying.

But lately Jesus' talk had turned to grimmer subjects. He was headed to Jerusalem, into the teeth of the opposition; he knew he would die there. The disciples were probably so much in denial that they missed his prediction of a joyous resurrection. Now they were in Jerusalem, and here at this Passover supper, Jesus was speaking again about love. The Father loved Jesus, Jesus loved the Father, and they both loved the disciples. Jesus said he was a "vine" and they were all "branches," connected to him, drawing nourishment from him—another one of Jesus' great word pictures.

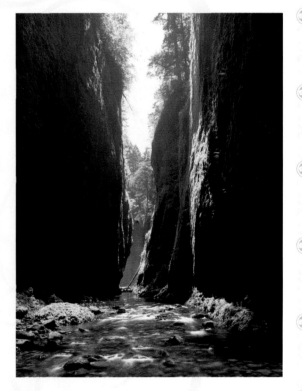

Joy is not gush; joy is not jolliness. Joy is perfect acquiescence in God's will because the soul delights in God himself.

H. W. WEBB-PEPLOE

Happiness is a sort of atmosphere you can live in sometimes when you're lucky. Joy is a light that fills you with hope and faith and love.

ADELA ROGERS ST. JOHNS

Why was he saying all this? So that their joy would be complete. Apparently the wonders of following Jesus were just the beginning of the good news. There was another shoe to drop. They would be spiritually tied with Jesus through all eternity, loving him and being loved. The joy of this relationship would lead them to the cross, to the tomb, and beyond—to a stunning reunion with the risen Lord. Their joy would carry them out to the world in ministry and ultimately to heaven in triumph. Their joy would be truly complete.

For modern-day disciples, there is much joy in pondering Jesus' teachings and watching him work in people's lives. But our joy begins to be complete when we connect with him, as a branch to the vine, tied to him in love.

Joy is not the same as pleasure or happiness. A wicked and evil man may have pleasure, while any ordinary mortal is capable of being happy. Pleasure generally comes from things, and always through the senses; happiness comes from humans through fellowship. Joy comes from loving God and neighbor. Pleasure is quick and violent, like a flash of lightning. Joy is steady and abiding, like a fixed star. Pleasure depends on external circumstances, such as money, food, travel, etc. Joy is independent of them, for it comes from a good conscience and love of God.

BISHOP FULTON J. SHEEN

JOY IN THE MORNING

When a woman is in labor, she has pain, because her hour has come. But when her child is born, she no longer remembers the anguish because of the joy of having brought a human being into the world. So you have your pain now, but I will see you again, and your hearts will rejoice, and no one will take your joy from you.

JOHN 16:21–22

IKE MANY COUPLES having their children in the 1970s and 1980s, my wife and I did the natural childbirth thing. We took Lamaze classes; we saw the whole thing as a bonding experience. But we went one step further than our friends—we had all four of our children with a midwife, two of them at home.

Although we know many fine, devoted medical people, Katie felt hospitals intruded unnecessarily into a natural process. And for a time she entertained the idea that childbirth could be painless, even without drugs. That was before she actually had a baby.

Since I'm the dad and not the mom, I really have no idea what kind of pain she experienced. But I do know she worked really hard. That's why they call it labor. She groaned and cried and screamed. She even bit my arm once. And when it was all over, she was physically and emotionally exhausted.

I especially remember our son Michael's birth. Katie had a short but intense labor, about five hours. When he was finally born, about 8:00 in the morning, he was purple. "Breathe, baby, breathe," the midwife said. When he did, we all did. It was a very happy moment.

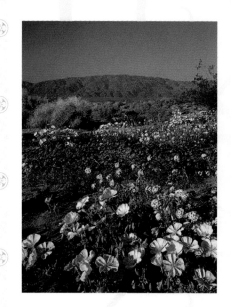

I held him, and then his sister, ten at the time, dressed him and put him in the cradle. Katie was too exhausted even to pick him up. But later that morning, after we all had recovered, she held him and nursed him. Once we put that baby in her arms, she didn't for a moment resent the effort it took to get him here.

Her mom was there and so was her sister. That evening I took the kids out in the yard and we set off some fireworks. We had a loud and joyous celebration, and we praised God for a new and healthy boy. It was certainly worth the work. Just to look at him made our hearts pound with excitement and gratitude.

Christ said the joy we will experience when he returns will be something like that. Our work to extend his kingdom in the world will be rewarded. Our hearts will rejoice, and no one will be able to take away our joy. That should be a loud and joyous celebration too, one that will last for a very long time.

* * *

JOY TO THE WORLD! THE LORD IS COME

Joy to the world! The Lord is come;
let earth receive her King;
let ev'ry heart prepare him room,
and heav'n and nature sing.

Joy to the earth! The Savior reigns;
let all their songs employ;
while field and floods, rocks, hills, and plains
repeat the sounding joy.

No more let sins and sorrows grow,
nor thorns infest the ground;
he comes to make his blessing flow
far as the curse is found.

He rules the world with truth and grace,
and makes the nations prove
the glories of his righteousness,
and wonders of his love.

ISAAC WATTS

*Lord,
I appreciate all the work you
went through to make me your
child. And I'm willing to work
now because I know I will see
you later. Give me both now
and then your everlasting joy.
Amen.*

THE BLESSED MORROW

'Midst the darkness, storm and sorrow,
One bright gleam I see;
Well I know the blessed morrow
Christ will come for me.
'Midst the light, and peace, and glory
Of the father's home,
Christ for me is watching, waiting,
Waiting till I come.

Long the blessed guide has led me
By the desert road;
Now I see the golden towers,
City of my God.
There amidst the love and glory,
He is waiting yet;
Of his hands a name is graven
He can ne'er forget.

There, amidst the songs of heaven
Sweeter to His ear
Is the footfall through the desert,
Ever drawing near.

There, made ready are the mansions,
Radiant, still and fair;
But the bride the Father gave Him
Yet is wanting there.

Who is this who comes to meet me
On the desert way,
As the morning Star foretelling
God's unclouded day?
He it is who came to win me
On the cross of shame;
In His glory well I know Him
Evermore the same.

Of the blessed joy of meeting,
All the desert past!
Oh the wondrous words of greeting
He shall speak at last!
He and I together entering
Those fair courts above—
He and I together sharing
All the Father's love.

Where no shade nor stain can enter,
Nor the gold be dim,
In that holiness unsullied,
I shall walk with Him.
Meet companion then for Jesus,
From Him, for Him, made—
Glory of God's grace for ever
There in me displayed.

He who in His hour of sorrow
Bore the curse alone;
I who through the lonely desert
Trod where He had gone;
He and I, in that bright glory,
One deep joy shall share—
Mine to be forever with Him;
His, that I am there.

GERHARD TERSTEEGEN

THREE HOLY WORDS

For the kingdom of God is not food and drink
but righteousness and peace and joy in the Holy Spirit.

ROMANS 14:17

THREE IS OFTEN THOUGHT OF as a holy number. The Gospel of Matthew records three gifts for baby Jesus brought by three kings (at least tradition says there were three). A more central tenet of the Christian faith is the Trinity of Father, Son, and Holy Spirit. In 1 Corinthians 13, Paul writes about faith, hope, and love. Here in Romans, we encounter another holy three—righteousness, peace, and joy.

Paul is writing to the Christians in Rome, urging them not to judge one another. Many new people are joining the newly established Christian church and bringing different traditions about eating, drinking, and fasting. The Jews who became Christians still felt there were some foods one should not eat—this was part of their upbringing. Yet in Christianity there is freedom to eat and drink whatever God has created, and non-Jewish Christians wanted to do so. So there were tensions, and Paul wanted them to remember that

Christian freedom goes together with Christian compassion. In other words, take into account other people and their faith as you go about practicing your own.

The holy three that Paul lifts up as guides are righteousness, peace, and joy. These are to be central for Christian practice and will give shape to discussions about food and drink, which are also important as the new community practices hospitality.

Righteousness is not a word we use often in modern-day conversation, yet it is a word with great tradition and meaning. It has to do with right relationships—with people and with God. The prophet Amos also has God decrying empty festivals and proclaiming, "Let justice roll down like waters, and righteousness like an ever flowing stream" (Amos 5:24). Righteousness means integrity, honesty, and compassion in all relationships. Paul says that it is to be the hallmark of the new church, that it takes into consideration the needs or weaknesses of other people.

Peace in the Bible is not just the absence of trouble but also the presence of well-being for the individual

and for the community. Peace is not a negative thing but an intensely positive thing; it is where harmony and open discussion foster peace. Jesus brings peace. He said, "Peace I leave with you, my peace I give to you" (John 14:27) and "Peace be with you" (John 20:21). As the new church centered itself on Jesus, Paul said that peace would prevail in the new community.

Lastly, Paul says your community should be hallmarked by joy. Jesus is the bringer of joy. "I have said these things to you so that my joy may be in you (John 15:11). The Holy Spirit is a preserver of joy, bringing warmth and surprises, coming like fire to stir us up and coming like wind to set our feet to dancing.

May your life be characterized by righteousness, peace, and joy.

For Jesus, peace seems to have meant not the absence of struggle but the presence of love.
FREDERICK BUECHNER, *WISHFUL THINKING: A THEOLOGICAL ABC*

Happiness turns up more or less where you'd expect it to—a good marriage, a rewarding job, a pleasant vacation. Joy, on the other hand, is as notoriously unpredictable as the one who bequeaths it.
FREDERICK BUECHNER, *WISHFUL THINKING: A THEOLOGICAL ABC*

A ROADSIDE REFUGE

*But let all who take refuge in you rejoice; let them ever sing
for joy. Spread your protection over them, so that those
who love your name may exult in you.*

PSALM 5:11

IT'S ABOUT A 20-MINUTE DRIVE to church from our house, winding through the flat open country of southern Michigan, past several farms. We often see a number of exotic animals on the way. There is a buffalo ranch and another farm where llamas and miniature horses are raised. Occasionally we see deer cross the road, and over the last ten years we've even hit a couple as they dart from the woods into the path of our car.

One of the delightful things we see each year is a pair of Canadian geese near a pond close beside the road. It's a swampy area, and the distance from the pavement to the water itself is no more than 15 feet. Each year these same geese, who mate for life, return to nest in that small space between

Are not two sparrows sold for a penny? Yet not one of them will fall to the ground apart from your Father. And even the hairs of your head are counted. So do not be afraid; you are of more worth than many sparrows.

JESUS CHRIST, *MATTHEW 10:29*

the road and the pond. And each spring we see five or six newly hatched goslings flocking around the mother while the father stands guard.

It's a difficult job I know—as a dad with little goslings of my own. But this family has picked a bad spot. There is another pond across the road, and each week we watch as the number of little geese decreases. Some are hit by cars, and others fall prey to the many natural predators nearby—raccoons, snakes, snapping turtles, and foxes. By the time the parents head south for the winter there is often nothing left of their little brood.

The whole little flock always seems anxious and fearful. Last Sunday the geese were out with their babies, and I turned the car around and drove back so the kids could get a closer look. The mother hurried them off, down to the edge of the pond, while the father came right out toward our van, neck extended, yelling at us in goose talk.

Yesterday, however, we went to town and saw a strange but amazing sight. In a deep drainage ditch between two parking lots, across the road from one of the area's department stores, we saw three pair of Canadian geese with 16 goslings between them.

We stopped to watch, and they didn't even notice us. These were happy geese making happy sounds, unruffled by the passing world. What was the difference between the city flock and the country flock? No predators, for one thing. The ditch opens into a marsh, but for the most part the creatures that might harm them stay far away from the strong scent of humans.

Another difference is that there isn't any reason to cross the road, no greener grass to lure them into the traffic. So their drainage ditch is a refuge of sorts, a personal paradise in the middle of a concrete world. The real difference is that the parents had picked the right spot.

It's good to know that our heavenly Father has picked the right spot for us, too. As Jesus reminded us, if the Father knows when a sparrow falls from a tree, he most certainly knows and cares about our fears and failures. "Look at the birds of the air," Jesus said. "They neither sow nor reap nor gather into barns, and yet your heavenly Father feeds them. Are you not of much more value than they?" (Matthew 6:26).

In a hurried, hectic world, he knows that place beside the road where we are safe. Like the young goslings, those who take refuge in him rejoice and sing for joy. The goslings are not songbirds, of course, and neither am I. But I can and should praise God for my refuge by the road.

❀ ❀ ❀ ❀

Lord,
I'm glad that you picked the spot where I can hide.
Please show it to me today, and give me joy.
Amen.

❀ ❀ ❀ ❀

THIS IS MY FATHER'S WORLD

This is my Father's world,
and to my list'ning ears
all nature sings and round me rings
the music of the spheres.
This is my Father's world;
I rest me in the thought

of rocks and trees, of skies and seas—
his hand the wonders wrought.

This is my Father's world:
God shines in all that's fair;
in rustling grass I hear him pass—
he speaks to me everywhere.
This is my Father's world:
Why should my heart be sad?
The Lord is King,
let heaven ring!
God reigns; let earth be glad.

MALTBIE BABCOCK

The foxes have holes, the birds of the air have nests, but you had no where to lay your head, O Lord. And yet you were a hiding place where the sinner could flee. Today you are still such a hiding place, and I flee to you. I hide myself under your wings, and your wings cover a multitude of my sins.

SOREN KIERKEGAARD

ADD BRIGHTNESS

*I will be glad and exult in you; I will sing
praise to your name, O Most High.*

PSALM 9:2

BRITISH BIBLE SCHOLAR William Barclay had to chuckle when he saw a detergent ad with only two words: *Adds brightness!* "I don't know if there could be a better definition of the effect of the Christian life," he commented. "If a person is a true Christian, he or she will add brightness everywhere."

Suzy is a person like that. When she agreed to play piano for a brand-new church, she didn't know what she was getting into. Her regular involvement with the church deepened her relationship with God, and that ignited her joyous heart. Whenever she played or sang or talked she overflowed with joy. It was contagious. The church's music was upbeat and down-to-earth; it came from hearts that were excited about the Lord. The whole church became a place where people enjoyed themselves, enjoyed one another, and rejoiced in God.

Not that everything was hunky-dory all the time. As Suzy grew in her faith, she realized she had to break up with a boyfriend who felt threatened by her newfound fervor. That was difficult. Later there were health problems in her family that caused her great concern. But joy isn't built on the ups and downs of our lives, it's based on our relationship with God. No matter the circumstances, God is constant, showing us love and energizing our hearts. As Suzy keeps connecting with him, her life radiates with an exultant joy.

Maybe you're not as bubbly as Suzy, but God promises to bring joy to your life, too. It could be a big celebration or a quiet satisfaction, but it's rooted in the amazing goodness of our loving Lord.

When I think of God, my heart is so full of joy that the notes leap and dance as they leave my pen: and since God has given me a cheerful heart, I serve him with a cheerful spirit.

FRANZ JOSEPH HAYDN

JOYFUL, JOYFUL, WE ADORE THEE

Joyful, joyful, we adore thee, God of glory, Lord of love;
hearts unfold like flow'rs before thee,
    op'ning to the sun above.
Melt the clouds of sin and sadness,
    drive the dark of doubt away;
giver of immortal gladness, fill us with the light of day.

All thy works with joy surround thee,
    earth and heav'n reflect thy rays,
stars and angels sing around thee,
    center of unbroken praise.
Field and forest, vale and mountain,
    flowery meadow, flashing sea,
chanting bird and flowing fountain,
    call us to rejoice in thee.

Thou art giving and forgiving, ever blessing, ever blest,
wellspring of the joy of living,
    ocean depth of happy rest!
Thou our Father, Christ our brother,
    all who live in love are thine;
teach us how to love each other, lift us to the joy divine.

HENRY VAN DYKE

Lord,
I thank you
for the joy you
bring me each day,
for the trials that test my joy,
for the comfort you
give when I'm tested,
for the love you show when
you comfort me,
for the joy I feel, knowing I'm
loved by you.
Lord, I thank you.
Amen.

FILL ME WITH YOUR JOY

You show me the path of life. In your presence there is fullness of joy; in your right hand are pleasures forevermore.

PSALM 16:11

A RETREAT LEADER was teaching a group of us a new way to pray based on an old tradition in the church. In the sixth century, a pilgrim seeking to grow closer to God was told to visit other monasteries to ask their guidance, and to pray, as he walked, some words that combined the prayer of the tax collector in Luke 18:13 (God, be merciful to me, a sinner) and an early confession of the church (Jesus is Lord). The words together were known as the "Jesus Prayer"—"Lord Jesus Christ, Son of God, have mercy on me, a sinner." As the pilgrim walked, prayed, and talked, over the years he changed. The prayer descended from his lips to his heart, and, because he had become a holy person, people now asked him to help them get closer to God.

The retreat leader said we could all develop our own prayer based on the Jesus Prayer (or use the Jesus prayer or a verse of scripture). He said the Jesus Prayer has

two main parts, a prayer of adoration or praise and a prayer of petition. To shape our own prayers, he asked us to find a name or prayer name for God and to imagine God in front of us, asking for our deepest desire. Take the name for God and the petition, and shape it into a six- or eight-sylla-ble phrase to create a breath prayer. Practice it so that every time you breathe, you are praying.

In the time the leader gave us to discover our breath prayer, I thought of eight or ten things that I wanted to say—which made my breath prayer much too long. I would hyperventilate trying to get all that in one breath. I asked the retreat leader about it, and he asked, "How would you feel if all that you desire were to come true?" I said, "I would feel happy, joyful!" He said, "That is what God wants for you—to be filled with joy."

For many years now I have been praying, "Loving God, fill me with your joy." I am convinced that God wants joy for all of us. In the presence of God "there is fullness of joy." Our desire for God and God's desire for us meet at a place called joy.

To be filled with joy is to know the presence of God. The joy of seeing a long-lost friend, the joy of a child's first birthday party, the joy of finishing an arduous hike are all ways we connect with God. God delights in seeing humans enjoying the blessings and pleasures of life. God created a beautiful, pleasing world and rejoices when we take delight in the smell of a rose, the beauty of a crescent moon, the tenderness of a baby's grasp, the sweetness of a ripe strawberry. Our joy and God's joy weave a strong fabric of faith.

God wants us to be joyful, to walk on the path of joy, to let joy reside in a deep place. Joy lasts longer than happiness, does not require money or expensive purchases, and is discovered in the simple acts of kindness, the hidden acts of care, the ordinary deeds of compassion. Let us receive God's promise of joy.

BE SURPRISED BY JOY

Be glad in the Lord and rejoice, O righteous,
and shout for joy, all you upright in heart.

PSALM 32:11

HAVE YOU SEEN *SHADOWLANDS?* It's a movie based on the life of British scholar C. S. Lewis. More specifically, it's based on his relationship with Joy Davidman, an American he eventually married.

Lewis was a Christian, and his writings instructed and inspired many believers. His philosophical arguments wooed many to the faith. He had a lot of things figured out. But not love. And not joy.

Oh, he had written brilliantly on these subjects, but he didn't open his heart to them. It was this woman, appropriately named Joy, who ambushed his emotions. It took a while to get through to him. Their relationship was professional, then platonic, and then it took a life-threatening illness (hers) to win him over. As he opened his heart to her, he felt great pain but also joy like he had never known before.

The lessons for us are many. First, love and joy seem to be intertwined. As we fully realize God's love for us (or another person's love), we respond with joy. Then our joy erupts with love in return.

Second, joy is never far from pain. In fact, sometimes it takes pain knifing through our hearts to get us ready to feel true joy. This sounds odd, but it's true. Joy is not the sheltered bliss of someone who has never faced tragedy but the seasoned satisfaction of one who has come through hard times. Even today's joy-filled verse comes from Psalm 32, which starts by talking about forgiveness. There is great joy in having your sins atoned for.

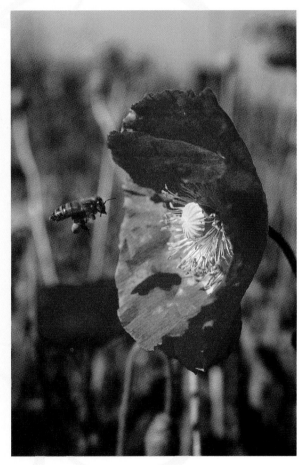

Finally, joy surprises us. We seldom go looking for it. We turn a corner and there it is, dazzling us—unless, of course, we're guarding against it. Too many people try to keep joy out of their lives. They don't like surprises, so they don't take chances. They don't like pain, so they avoid loving anyone or anything too much. And their lives are much poorer for it.

Let joy surprise you today.

*Mirth is the sweet wine of human life. It should be offered,
sparkling with zestful life, unto God.*

HENRY WARD BEECHER

*"On with the dance, let the joy be unconfined!" is my motto,
whether there's any dance to dance or any joy to unconfine.*

MARK TWAIN

REJOICE, THE LORD IS KING!

Rejoice, the Lord is King! Your Lord and King adore!

Rejoice, give thanks, and sing, and triumph evermore:

Lift up your heart, lift up your voice!

Rejoice, again I say, rejoice!

Our Savior, Jesus, reigns, the God of truth and love;

when he had purged our stains, he took his seat above:

Lift up your heart, lift up your voice!

Rejoice, again I say, rejoice!

Rejoice in glorious hope for Christ the Judge shall come

to gather all his saints to their eternal home:

Lift up your heart, lift up your voice!

Rejoice, again I say, rejoice!

CHARLES WESLEY

GOD PROMISES COMFORT

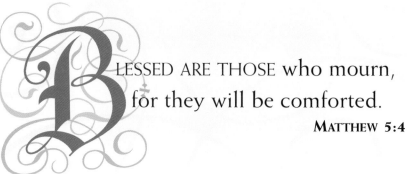

LESSED ARE THOSE who mourn,
for they will be comforted.

MATTHEW 5:4

REST AND COMFORT UNDER THE SHEPHERD'S CARE

The Lord is my shepherd, I shall not want. He makes me lie down in green pastures; he leads me beside still waters; he restores my soul. He leads me in right paths for his name's sake. Even though I walk through the darkest valley, I fear no evil; for you are with me; your rod and your staff—they comfort me.

PSALM 23:1–4

I DON'T THINK I have ever been to a funeral where Psalm 23 was not used. This psalm has given so much comfort to those who are mourning. Yet, if we use this passage only at funerals, we miss the comfort and wisdom that it offers for everyday living.

God is like a shepherd who knows us; he takes care of our needs. That affirmation begins the psalm. Though shepherds worked long and hard, faced many difficulties, and ranked at the lower end of the social scale, we tend to have positive, pastoral images of them. We are comforted that Jesus called himself a shepherd: "I am the good shepherd. I know my own and my own know me" (John 10:14).

God invites us to rest, whether in green pastures or beside still streams. In our busy society, we often only dream of truly resting. I read a study of office workers that said in a given day they receive or send 177 messages. Memos, faxes, e-mail, beepers, phone calls, call forwarding, even letters. We are more in touch and more overwhelmed than ever before.

New technologies come and are quickly replaced with something even newer. But we don't always have the ability to cope with all the information accosting us and to respond to all that is demanded of us. People assume that because e-mail is almost instantaneous, we should instantly answer all e-mail  messages. The speed of communication has left us floundering and searching for ways to reply that do not violate the human spirit. In the midst of our global village, the psalmist invites us to rest, restore our soul, and find comfort.

We can turn off our pagers, sleep in late, take a walk, smell the flowers, linger over a meal. We can sit beside a river and listen to the sound of water dancing around the stones. We can look at the trees reaching toward the sky and feel our spirits stretching toward the heavens. Several times I have come close to burnout. I have

been overcommitted and have experienced what a friend calls "compassion fatigue." One of the first remedies for burnout is rest. I take some time each day for myself; I take some time each week, not just for errands and catching up on the long list of things to do, but for really healing and renewing. The Hebrews called it *sabbath*. They took a day to prepare so that on sabbath, they would not have to do work. They could give themselves over to worship, study, prayer, and family. They could take time to restore their souls and refocus their direction. They could remind themselves that God was a shepherd who cared for them, who led them to freedom from captivity, and who took them beside still waters.

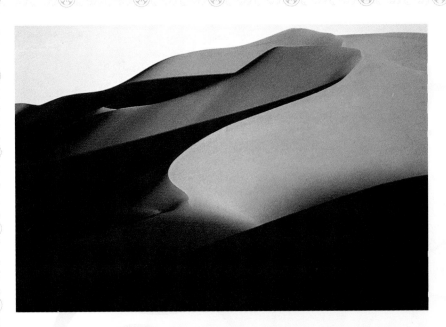

Beside taking time each day and each week, counselors suggest there should be yearly vacations and periodic sabbaticals. These should be part of every person's life, not just those in academia. Who of us would not benefit from three months to six months time to retool, reinvigorate? When I read these verses from Psalm 23, I am reminded of the human need to rest, and I know I must be intentional about structuring those times—daily, weekly, yearly.

The psalm shifts from resting to moving. God cares about the directions we are going. God wants to lead us on "right paths," paths of honesty, integrity, kindness,

A cheap, second-class religion offers the pious message: "Fear not. If you love God and trust in God, none of those things you fear will happen to you." A good religion, on the other hand says: "Fear not! All of those things you dread may very well happen to you. However, they're nothing of which you need to be afraid. With God's grace you will overcome each of them."

ED HAYS, *THE ASCENT OF THE MOUNTAIN OF GOD*

and compassion. Each morning I ask God to guide me through the meetings and events coming that day. I trust the words of the psalm—God wants to lead me.

There are days and events that are dark valleys, and even then the psalmist assures us that God is present. God's presence casts out fear and provides us with comfort. It is these verses that people hold onto in the midst of grief. The King James translation of the Bible calls this the "valley of the shadow of death." All of us walk through that valley at some time in our life. After a memorial service for a young boy who had drowned, people in our city came up to me and said, "I am really shaken by this tragedy. I can't stop crying, but people in your church seem to be doing better than I am. Why?" People in our church were equally devastated by the death, but they had a faith to see them through; they believed in the words of Psalm 23: "I fear no evil; for you are with me; your rod and your staff—they comfort me." They shed tears, but they knew the comfort of the shepherd.

I believe we shall continue to read Psalm 23 at every funeral, and, I hope, it will be our daily companion as well.

LAY YOUR BURDENS DOWN

Come to me, all you that are weary and are carrying heavy burdens, and I will give you rest. Take my yoke upon you, and learn from me; for I am gentle and humble in heart, and you will find rest for your souls. For my yoke is easy, and my burden is light.
MATTHEW 11:28–30

JESUS KNEW what a yoke was. He and Joseph probably made them in their carpenter's shop. Basically, a yoke is a wooden frame placed over the neck of two oxen and attached to a plow, sled, or cart. It was different than a harness used on a horse; the yoke was designed to pull against the broad, strong shoulders of a draft animal.

But Jesus knew what a yoke was in a figurative sense, too. For centuries, yokes had been used on captives and slaves, and the prophets had compared the oppression Israel experienced as a "yoke of bondage." Hardship and forced labor, servitude and submission: These hardships were not unknown to this tiny nation at the crossroads of the ancient world.

Jesus and his followers had experienced all this at the hands of the Romans. High taxes—without representation—was only one form of oppression. Cruel punishments, including crucifixion, were meted out daily. All a Roman soldier had to do was ask, and a Jew had to carry his baggage for a mile.

But Jesus was aware—and concerned—about another yoke of bondage. The law itself, the moral precepts God had given his people, had become bogged down in sometimes meaningless ritual and minutia. The people were oppressed not only by Roman legion but also by some Jewish leaders. Jesus seemed more concerned about money changers and some pharisees than he was about the Romans.

It must have come as quite a surprise when he offered his followers another yoke, however. And it was an offer he made to those who were already weary and carrying heavy burdens. "Take my yoke," he said, "and you will find rest."

What did this mean to the simple peasants and farmers who flocked around him? He was saying that, in contrast to the teaching of the scribes, his way was easy. He taught that all the law could be simply summarized: "Love the Lord your God with all your heart, and love your neighbor as yourself."

The simplicity of his call was truly liberating to those who were willing to listen. And to us, too. This is because the bondage most of us experience is to our-selves. To act in our own interests is complicated. We often find ourselves enmeshed in a web of deception and mistrust. We don't know what to do, and we worry about what others will think.

But as we focus on God and others, we find life is much less stressful. Our choices become clearer, our lives happier. We find the rest our anxious spirits crave. Compared to a life of self-ish ambition, or even of Roman occupation, God's way is less wearisome, and his burden is much lighter.

His yoke is easy for another reason, too. It isn't just comparatively easier. It really is just easier. That's because we work willingly for what we love. You might

FREEDOM AND FAITH

For love makes all, the hardest and most distressing things, altogether easy.... The things which are hard to those that labor lose their roughness to the same men when they love. Wherefore it has been so arranged by the dispensation of Divine goodness, that to the "inner man who is renewed day by day," placed no longer under the Law but under Grace, and freed from the numberless observances which were indeed a heavy yoke, every grievous trouble should, through the easiness of simple faith, and a good hope, and holy charity, become light through the joy within.

St. Augustine of Hippo

work ten times harder playing basketball or weeding your garden than you do when you're cleaning the house; you don't complain a bit if it's something you love to do.

Jesus isn't saying that following him will be without its difficulties. In fact, in other places he says we might even have a cross of our own to bear. But he is saying that as we experience his gentle and humble heart, we will love him. Then our yoke will be easy and our burdens will be light. And that's a promise.

*Lord,
You have promised me rest. You have promised that following you will be easier than following myself. Today, please teach me your gentle and humble ways, and help me rest in your promise as I gladly accept your yoke.
Amen.*

A GOOD CONFESSION

The chains that have bound me are flung to the wind,
by the mercy of God the poor slave is set free.
And the strong arm of heaven breathes fresh
    o'er the mind,
like the bright winds of summer that brighten the sea.

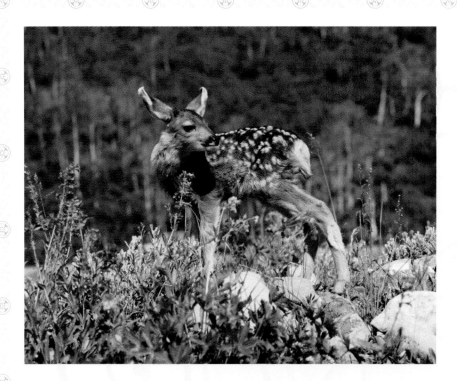

I cried out in mercy, and fell on my knees,

and confessed, while my heart with keen sorrow was

    wrung;

'twas the labor of minutes, and years of disease

fell as fast from my soul as the words from my tongue.

And now, blest be God and the sweet Lord who died!

No deer on the mountain, no bird in the sky,

no dark wave that leaps on the dark bounding tide,

is a creature so free or so happy as I.

FREDERICK WILLIAM FARBER

AN IMMOVABLE FORCE

Cast your burden on the Lord, and he will sustain you;
he will never permit the righteous to be moved.

PSALM 55:22

THIS VERSE is a favorite of couch potatoes. They like the idea that God will never permit them to be moved. But that's not exactly what the psalmist had in mind.

Think instead of the elderly couple who have lived in their home for 50 years. Then the state highway commission announces it wants to build a new road—right through their home. The couple want to keep their home, but the commission puts pressure on them, first offering money, then threats. But the couple stubbornly refuse to give up their home, and they pray for strength to withstand the opposition. Finally, the road is built elsewhere—they would not be moved.

Or picture this: UPS delivers a huge box to your company, and you have to haul it up to your fifth-floor office. Unfortunately, the elevators aren't working, so you're carrying it up the steps. At the fourth-floor landing you start to totter. Your weary knees are buckling, and you're losing your grip. You're about to do a header down four flights, with this huge box tumbling right behind you. But then Big Mac shows up, the biggest guy in the mail room. "Here, let me help you with that," he says, and with one sweep of his brawny arms he grabs the box as if it were a child's toy. "You should have let me carry this to begin with."

We often carry burdens that are too big for us. Worries about our future. Guilt about our past. We suffer grief over lost friends and lost opportunities. Sometimes we feel as if we will fall under the weight of all our woes.

But God is there to help us. We can "cast our burdens on the Lord," and he will keep us from falling. Don't let that "righteous" term bother you. Certainly none of us is righteous compared to the Lord. But the psalmist is simply drawing a distinction between those who care about the Lord and those who don't. It's not about having a spotless life—then no one would have a chance—it's about trusting God to provide comfort in your times of crisis.

So let him carry the things that are weighing you down.

Lord God,

I'm sad. The happy times I've had before, well, they
    seem very far away right now.

I miss the friends who've died or moved.

I miss the life I used to have.

You have no idea how sad I feel.

...Oh, yeah, maybe you do.

Lord God,

I'm frustrated. Life isn't turning out the way I wanted.

I fail when I desperately want to succeed. Again and
    again.

I thought there would be so much more—at work, in
    my family, in my community, in my church—
    but it's just not there.

I don't get any breaks.

Do you have any clue how I'm feeling right now?

...Oh, yes, I guess you do.

Lord God,

I'm angry. My friends have let me down.

I trusted them, and they put their own needs first,
    forgetting about me.

I feel lonely now and really mad. Only I have no one

How often we look upon God as our last and feeblest resource! We go to him because we have nowhere else to go. And then we learn that the storms of life have driven us, not upon the rocks, but into the desired haven.

GEORGE MACDONALD

Lord, either lighten my burden or strengthen my back.

THOMAS FULLER

left to tell about it.

Could you possibly know what it's like to be betrayed
by your closest friends, to have them act as if they
don't know you?

. . . On second thought, you probably could.

Lord God,

I need your comfort. I need
to feel your strong arms
embracing me.

I don't need wise words or
brilliant truth—just *be*
there for me now.

Remind me of your love
for me. Tell me
everything's going to
be all right.

Assure me again that you know what I'm going through,
because you've been there.

You have felt my pain, and now you can share it.

Thank you for sitting with me through this crisis.

I praise you for your awesome love.

Amen.

THREE CROSSES ON THE WATER

Do not let your hearts be troubled.
Believe in God, believe also in me.
JOHN 14:1

ONE SUNDAY, a very striking mother and daughter visited our church. In conversation with them after the worship service I learned that the young woman was a singer from another part of the country, but she had not come west to sing. Cheri and her mother had come so she could receive a special kind of chemotherapy for her melanoma. Her mother had rented out their East Coast apartment and journeyed with Cheri to be her support person. While they were at the hospital, one of the counselors said, "You both are going to need a lot of support for Cheri's difficult treatment. Do you have a faith background, some religious community that can give you spiritual support?" They were not regular churchgoers, but they had some church contact, so they agreed to look for a church in their new short-term community. Somehow God led them to our church community.

Over the next few months, I visited them in the hospital and at their apartment. They were wonderfully talented and creative individuals, very artistic and musical. They were ready to try anything to help stop the spread of cancer. We talked of prayer and meditation. They changed their diet. They went to support groups. They got exercise and surrounded themselves with beauty—in nature, in art.

Still, the cancer progressed and took its toll on Cheri. The mother had already lost two husbands to death and was fighting to keep her only child. At times she would rail against God. "How can you let this happen? It is not fair!" Other times she would plead. "God, take me, not my lovely daughter who has so much to give." Her prayers reminded me of the psalms, so passionate, so filled with feeling, so anguished. Her love and will were astounding. I sat awed at her strength. I held her when she cried and listened when she prayed. I shared her anguish. I added my prayers.

When Cheri died, I was away at a conference. When I got the call I felt my heart sink at the news. The mother was going to fly back to the East Coast for the funeral, and she wanted me to come and lead the funeral service because she had no home church. I made plans to leave my responsibilities early and fly east. All the way there I wondered what I would say to her friends and relatives who were filled with such grief and anger.

I wanted to speak words of comfort and hope. "Do not let your hearts be troubled." Whatever feelings you have, acknowledge them but do not let them dominate your heart. Do not lose sight of the joy in Cheri's life. Do not lose touch with a God who is bigger than death. Do not let your feelings obscure the compassion you can show to one another now and every day.

"Believe in God, believe also in me." I tried to point them in the direction of God. I wanted them to look up from death and see the comfort God promises. This passage in John goes on to talk about the rooms that God has prepared for us, for Cheri. I hoped they would not let death rob them of their belief in God, who sustains us in life and in death. It was one of the hardest sermons I have ever given. I know the mother was grateful for my message, but she still had so many doubts after three significant losses.

Many months later, I learned the mother was back
west to settle the closing of the apartment. I spoke with
her, and she told me that the night before she had
looked out the apartment window and had seen some
boats in the ocean, fishing at night. When she looked
back several minutes later, she saw three lighted crosses

whose beams shone across
the water right into her
room. She thought of the
crucifixion story. I asked
her about the three deaths
in her life. She said she
had felt a great peace
wash over her when she
saw the crosses. The first
real peace since Cheri's
death. I said, "God even
uses the rigging of three
fishing boats to send you a message. It seems that God
is not through with you yet. God is still at work sustain-
ing you."

Do not let your hearts be troubled. Believe in God,
believe also in me.

THIS TRAIN IS BOUND FOR GLORY

And I will ask the Father, and he will give you another
Advocate, to be with you forever. I will not leave you orphaned;
I am coming to you.

JOHN 14:16,18

THE POOR IMMIGRANTS coming to the United States in the late 19th century left poverty and oppression, looking for a better life. Unfortunately for many, life didn't improve much.

There were few jobs, and if they did find one, there weren't any labor unions, sick leave options, or insurance plans. Wages were low since there were many others willing to take their jobs. And, of course, there wasn't any assistance for those who were injured working in dangerous and often deplorable conditions.

Children whose parents could not or would not take care of them took to the streets, selling newspapers, begging, and stealing. By 1854, there were nearly 24,000 homeless children in New York City.

A young Methodist minister named Charles Brace decided he wasn't cut out to preach—but he could care for kids. He founded the Children's Aid Society of New York in 1853, and he started schools to teach kids the skills they needed to get jobs. Unfortunately, attendance was poor, and there was no way to place all the kids in orphanages.

So, Brace decided to send as many children as possible to live with farm families in the west. "In every American community, especially in a western one, there are spare places at the table of life," he wrote. "There is no harassing struggle for existence. They have enough for themselves and the stranger, too."

Brace sent announcements to Midwest towns announcing when a trainload of orphans would arrive. When the trains stopped, the children would be paraded before the crowd, and couples could choose a child.

The first "orphan train" stopped in Dowagiac, Michigan, in 1854, and the trains continued until 1929, traveling as far as Missouri. The Catholic Charities of New York also sent "mercy trains" west, to townx approved by the parish priests. As many as 400,000 children may have found homes in this way.

There were, of course, some instances of abuse and neglect. Some of the children who went west were forced into hard labor. But most of these children found homes where they were well treated and, in most cases, well loved.

Take Jessie Martin, of Hays, Kansas. She was taken to a Catholic hospital when she was only nine days old, and she went west to Kansas when she was four. She later learned that her parents had been Jewish. "They took all religions at the hospital," she says. "But you didn't leave until you were Catholic."

Today she wears a cross and a Star of David. "There was a time when I didn't have a relative in the world," she says. "Now I have 14 children and 29 grandchildren."

Or consider Irma, who arrived in Taos, Missouri, in 1901, just shy of her third birthday. Her foster family was German, so she had to learn a new language. But she was accepted by her community and grew up to be the valedictorian of her high school. She became a teacher, married, and raised eight children.

This heritage of the orphan trains is all because one man was willing to be an advocate for homeless children in New York City. He wasn't willing to let 24,000 kids live without homes—and without hope.

Jesus felt the same way. Even though he was returning to heaven, he told his disciples the night before he died that he would send an Advocate—the Holy Spirit—to look after our interests and his. He said the Spirit of God would be a Counselor and a Comforter.

On the so-called "gospel train" of the old southern hymn, we are bound for glory. "I will not leave you orphaned," Christ said.

He has promised to meet us at the train.

Lord,
I am glad to be your child.
Thank you for your Holy
Spirit, who watches over me.
Keep me safe until you come
for me, just as you promised.
Amen.

THE COMFORTER HAS COME

O spread the tidings 'round, wherever man is found, wherever human hearts and human woes abound; let every Christian tongue proclaim the joyful sound: The Comforter has come!

The Comforter has come, the Comforter has come!
The Holy Ghost from heaven,
    the Father's promise given;
O spread the tidings 'round, wherever man is found—
    the Comforter has come!

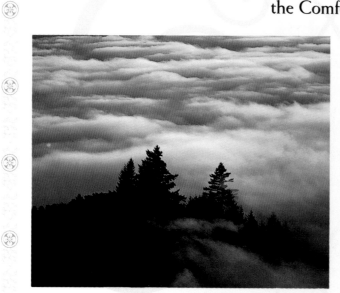

The long, long night is past, the morning
    breaks at last,
and hushed the dreadful wail and fury of
    the blast,
as over the golden hills the day advances
    fast!
The Comforter has come!

Lo, the great King of kings, with healing
    in his wings,
to every captive soul a full deliverance brings;
and through the vacant cells the song of triumph rings;
the Comforter has come!

O boundless love divine! How shall this tongue of mine
to wondering mortals tell the matchless grace divine—
that I, a child of hell, should in his image shine!
The Comforter has come!

FRANK BOTTOME

JOY IN THE MOURNING

Very truly, I tell you, you will weep and mourn, but the world will rejoice; you will have pain, but your pain will turn into joy.

JOHN 16:20

"LET'S TRY IT AGAIN." The student actor was getting more and more frustrated as the director called for yet another run-through of the scene. It was a crucial part of the school play, and the young star was just not showing enough emotion.

"Reach down deep inside yourself," the director coached, "and find your own feelings. Remember how you felt when you were in a situation like this. Then let those emotions out. Don't hold back."

The student tried to remember a similar scene from her life, struggling to picture the details, to recall the feelings. It was a major challenge, rolling through emotions of the past, then summoning them on cue and strongly delivering them to an audience.

"This is hard," she complained.

"You bet it's hard," the director snapped. "What? Did you think you'd just go on stage and say anything you felt like and then bask in the applause of your adoring fans? No way. This is work, like anything else in life. You have to get your hands dirty, digging for true emotions, and you have to give everything you've got to get those feelings out to your audience. It's very hard work, and don't you forget it."

It was perhaps the best thing the actress could have heard. She took the challenge and progressed nicely through many exhausting rehearsals. When she took her bow on opening night, she accepted the applause as payment for a job well done. It was work, but it was worth it. Her blood, sweat, and tears had turned to love, praise, and cheers.

Following Jesus isn't easy, either. Jesus promised an *abundant* life, not a peachy one. At the Last Supper he warned his disciples that in the world they would have trouble—but ultimately he would overcome. In John 16:20, things seem pretty bleak until the last word. Jesus' people are weeping while the world is making merry. But suddenly all that weeping turns to joy.

> *We must wait for God, long, meekly, in the wind and wet, in the thunder and lightning, in the cold and the dark. Wait, and he will come. He never comes to those who do not wait. He does not go their road. When he comes, go with him, but go slowly, fall a little behind; when he quickens his pace, be sure of it before you quicken yours. But when he slackens, slacken at once; and do not be slow only, but silent, very silent, for he is God.*
>
> **FREDERICK W. FABER**

Specifically, he was speaking about his upcoming death. Jesus' enemies would be glad that they had finally rid the world of this rabble-rouser, and Jesus' friends would mourn his death. Yet the tables would turn a few days later when Jesus came back to life. The disciples might wish to be spared the sorrow of Jesus' death, but without it there is no joy of resurrection.

The same holds true for us. We might wish for a life full of pleasant things, but Jesus warns us to expect sorrow. And sometimes we may experience difficulty *because* we follow Jesus. But don't give up hope. Crucifixion gives way to resurrection. Mourning turns to joy.

If we had no winter, the spring would not be so pleasant.
ANNE BRADSTREET

IT IS WELL WITH MY SOUL

When peace, like a river, attends my way,
when sorrows like sea billows roll;
whatever my lot, you have taught me to say,
"It is well, it is well with my soul."

Though Satan should buffet, though trials should come,
let this blest assurance control,
that Christ has regarded my helpless estate,
and has shed his own blood for my soul.

My sin—O the bliss of this glorious thought—
my sin, not in part, but the whole,
is nailed to the cross, and I bear it no more,
praise the Lord, praise the Lord, O my soul!

And, Lord, haste the day when my faith shall be sight,
the clouds be rolled back as a scroll,
the trumpet shall sound and the Lord shall descend,
even so—it is well with my soul.

HORATIO G. SPAFFORD

NO MORE TEARS

He will wipe every tear from their eyes. Death will be no more;
mourning and crying and pain will be no more,
for the first things have passed away.

REVELATION 21:4

WHAT CAUSES YOU to cry? Is it sadness for a child who leaves home? Is it the picture of a war-torn village or a starving child? Is it the death of a loved one? Is it a movie in a darkened theater that provides a safe place for your tears? Is it the word of a doctor who brings unwelcome news of serious illness? Tears are part of life. From a child's tears at the moment of cutting a finger to an adult's sobs at the funeral of a spouse. Tears flow from a deep place inside. Often they surprise us. We did not know the hurt, the loss, would affect us so much. Other times we worry that we are blocking our emotions by not shedding some tears. Tears.

God promises comfort for our times of sadness, pain, and grief, our times of tears. These promises of God are written in the image-filled, poetic writing of the last book in the Bible.

John, the writer of Revelation, was imprisoned on the Island of Patmos for his proclamation of the good news about Jesus Christ. While he was on the island he had a number of visions, images he received from God for the benefit of the growing number of Christian churches. He knew Christians were already being persecuted, and he believed that a more difficult time was yet to come.

He could see that tears and pain would come to Christians who did not fit into the status quo, who would not bow down to other gods—whether they be Caesar or money or social standing.

Near the end of Revelation, John writes of his vision of a new future for the churches. It is a vision of a new heaven and earth, where God will dwell with the people and comfort them, where God will wipe away tears and death, and where mourning and pain will be no more.

For people who were suffering, these are words of hope and comfort. God will be with them through their difficulties. The persecutions, trials, and temptations will not be the last word. Tears will not be the final ritual. God will bring comfort.

When my children were young, they would come running to me with tears in their eyes. They did not want me to say that they should not have tried to climb that tree. They did not want me to remind them to keep their fingers away from the closing car door. They wanted me to wipe away their tears, to hold them in their pain, and to promise them that it would get better and the future would be bright.

When you face difficulty, pain, or death, you do not need a scolding about what you should have done differently. What you want is the strong sense that God is with you. As you turn to God for help, you desire to hear what John was telling us, "God will wipe the tears from your eyes. Death, mourning, crying, and pain shall not trouble you any more."

READY TO WEAR

You have turned my mourning into dancing;
you have taken off my sackcloth and clothed me with joy.

PSALM 30:11

BRUCE MADE HIS LIVING traveling the world and writing books about his adventures. Intrepid, he would traipse deep through uncharted jungles or walk through a third-world revolution just to get a story. After one visit with a primitive tribe, he made a brief research stop in England before heading back to the United States. But one evening at a London pub, Bruce chatted with one of the locals about his exploits.

It turned out the man he was conversing with had many friends in the upper crust of British society. He offered Bruce the use of his home for a few days as he conducted his research. It would be great to have a real live explorer under his roof. And, by the way, the duchess had invited him and his wife to a formal dinner that weekend—would Bruce like to come along? The duchess would love to hear of Bruce's adventures.

This was quite a contrast for Bruce, who a week earlier had been sleeping under the stars with a stone-age tribe. Now he'd be noshing with nobility. He was about to accept the invitation when he realized he had nothing to wear. Of course he hadn't packed a tuxedo for his trip into the bush country. All the clothes he had in his suitcase bore the stains and tears of his recent journeys—certainly not duchess material.

"No matter," his host answered. "I'll buy you a suitable outfit." And so he did. A tailor was contacted, and by the weekend Bruce had a smart new suit in which to delight the duchess.

When the psalmist mentions sackcloth, he's referring to a coarse material worn in times of mourning or repentance. It wasn't pretty, and it didn't feel good to wear. That was the whole point. In such moments, even your attire should contribute to the feeling of sorrow. These definitely weren't party clothes.

But God invites us to a party! He comes to us when we're feeling down, and he says, "Let's dance."

"But I have nothing to wear," we protest.

No problem. He outfits us in joy.

So what are you mourning? A loss, a regret, a sense

JUST A THOUGHT

God promises us his comfort, but he also uses us as his agents to comfort others. In fact, the difficulties we've gone through often give us the ability to reassure others who are now going through the same experiences. How will God use you to extend comfort to someone else?

When you are in the dark, listen, and God will give you a very precious message for someone else when you get into the light.

OSWALD CHAMBERS

of guilt, growing frustration? It doesn't matter anymore. God wants to dance with you. Already he's putting his arm around you and helping you up. The music is playing and the Lord is moving.

Will you join in the dance? As you do, suddenly you realize that your mourning clothes have vanished, and the Lord has wrapped you in pure joy. The problems are left behind as you waltz across the dance floor. You are sparkling now, clothed in delight. When you're dancing with him, how can you wear anything else?

Your rod and your staff—they comfort me.

PSALM 23:4

Come, ye disconsolate, where'er ye languish,
come to the mercy seat, fervently kneel.
Here bring your wounded hearts, here tell your
 anguish:
Earth has no sorrow that heaven cannot heal.

Joy of the desolate, light of the straying,
hope of the penitent, fadeless and pure!
Here speaks the Comforter, tenderly saying,
"Earth has no sorrow that heaven cannot cure."

Here see the Bread of Life; see waters flowing
forth from the throne of God, pure from above.
Come to the feast of love; come, ever knowing
Earth has no sorrow but heaven can remove.

THOMAS MOORE
ADAPTED BY THOMAS HASTINGS

God does not comfort us to make us comfortable,
but to make us comforters.

JOHN HENRY JOWETT

GOD PROMISES STRENGTH

THE LORD IS the everlasting God, the Creator of the ends of the earth. He does not faint or grow weary; his understanding is unsearchable. He gives power to the faint, and strengthens the powerless. Even youths will faint and be weary, and the young will fall exhausted; but those who wait for the Lord shall renew their strength, they shall mount up with wings like eagles, they shall run and not be weary, they shall walk and not faint.

ISAIAH 40:28–31

STRENGTH IN PLACE OF FEAR

The Lord is my strength and my might;
he has become my salvation.

PSALM 118:14

A WOMAN CAME to see me about some troubling dreams. They would wake her up and make her afraid. She could not understand why they were happening to her. She had lived a good Christian life. She had been helpful in the church. Why was she being disturbed?

We talked some about the images in the dreams and what they could mean. We talked about waiting patiently for the meanings to unfold, but she was still agitated. I asked her about her prayer life. She had become so concerned about her dreams that she was not being faithful to her other spiritual practices. I encouraged her to restart her times of meditation, her regular church attendance, and I encouraged her to pray this verse, "The Lord is my strength and my might." Every time she felt nervous during the day, pray the verse. Each night before going to bed, pray the verse. She needed to call on the Lord's strength.

Another person was struggling as a writer, and when money ran low he took a part-time job helping autistic adults. It was something entirely new, and though he was a caring person, he had some doubts about working with this group of people. Over and over he said this verse until it had a resting place in his heart—it gives him confidence and strength. (He now is a director in a large agency working with multineed adults.)

While I was in college, I helped a neighborhood move toward integration. The community group I worked with met with realtors to ease the transition, but not all were cooperating with new Federal guidelines. On one occasion, I was confronted by an angry realtor, and I feared for my life. I wish I had memorized Psalm 118:14—I really needed God's help at that moment. Somehow we made it through that confrontation, and the neighborhood we worked in did not experience "white flight" and plummeting property values that many other neighborhoods experienced.

Most of us at some time or another find ourselves afraid. We feel the task ahead of us is too big or the injustice too complex and frightening. Doubts fill our minds, butterflies start flying inside of us, our muscles go limp. Psalm 118 is a good psalm to read at such a time. Remember, the Israelites had faced trouble that surrounded them on every side, but "the Lord helped" (verse 13) and "has become my salvation" (verse 14). The verses that follow are songs of praise and thanksgiving, for God does keep the promises that he will be our strength and our might. Thanks be to God.

NOW THANK WE ALL OUR GOD

Now thank we all our God
with hearts and hands and voices,
who wondrous things hath done,
in whom this world rejoices;
who, from our mothers' arms,
hath blessed us on our way
with countless gifts of love,
and still is ours today.

MARTIN RINKART
TRANSLATED BY CATHERINE WINKWORTH

PROMISE KEEPER

Turn to me and be gracious to me, for I am lonely and afflicted.
Relieve the troubles of my heart, and bring me out of my distress.
PSALM 25:16–17

I'S NOT ALWAYS EASY to be second. The second child gets hand-me-downs. The second chair in the orchestra is second fiddle. Hagar, however, had the unfortunate position of second wife, a concubine in a culture where women were already second class.

She was a slave girl, and she belonged to Abraham's wife, Sarah. After years of trying to have a son, Sarah finally sent Hagar to Abraham's tent, unwilling to wait for God to keep his promise of an heir.

This did elevate Hagar's status, however. Perhaps Abraham liked her and sent for her again and again. But the Bible says she began to despise her mistress, especially after becoming pregnant.

Sarah didn't like this new arrangement. She gave Abraham an ultimatum: "It's her or me." Abraham chose

Sarah. She was a beautiful woman, so beautiful that two kings tried to steal her from him. And besides, they had been through a lot together, years of looking for a place of promise and waiting for a son. So he said to Sarah, "It's up to you. Do whatever you think is best." Sarah began to put Hagar in her place. She mistreated her. She may have even beat her. She certainly made her a slave again; we can be sure there was no place for her in Abraham's tent. So Hagar ran away.

She was an Egyptian, so she headed out across the wilderness in the direction of Egypt, along the road to Shur. But she didn't get very far. It was hot, she was weak, and she apparently collapsed beside a spring in the desert.

We can imagine that her prayer was very much like the one we all pray at a time like that. The psalmist put it this way: "Turn to me and be gracious to me, for I am lonely and afflicted. Relieve the troubles of my heart, and bring me out of my distress."

It was there and then that an angel of the Lord appeared to her. "Where are you coming from, and where are you going?" he asked.

"I'm running away," she said.

The angel told her that wasn't a very good idea. "You are going to have a son," he said. "Go back home, and God will take care of you and bless you."

Alone in the desert, Hagar discovered a great truth. "I have now seen the one who sees me," she said. And she called the oasis where the angel appeared "A Well of the Living One Who Sees Me."

Hagar returned to Abraham, who loved her and their son. And later, when Sarah had a son of her own and sent Hagar away again, God heard Hagar's prayer and brought her to another well in the wilderness.

He kept his promise to her, as he does to us. He is the God who sees us and hears us, even when—or perhaps especially when—we are lonely and distressed.

Lord,
Thank you for listening to me
and watching me, even when I
am alone and lost in the desert.
Give me peace as I trust in your
promises, and give me not just a
drink of water but a well of
everlasting life.
Amen.

VERY HERE

God is our refuge and strength, a very present help in trouble.
PSALM 46:1

LITTLE JANIE HAD a book report to give to the whole class on Monday, and she was well prepared. Some kids might be nervous about this, but not Janie. All weekend she practiced, and Monday she rushed to school, eager to make her presentation. When roll was called, the students one by one answered, "Here"—until the teacher uttered Janie's name. But Janie was reviewing her notes, not paying attention.

"Janie," the teacher repeated. "Are you here?"

Jolted from her reading, the little girl blurted, "Yes, I'm very here!"

That's the phrase used for God in Psalm 46. God is not only present—here with us when we need him—he is very here. Like little Janie, he is eager to do his part.

You may experience times when you think God is absent. Certainly he has other prayers to answer, other children to attend to, other problems to solve. But then in the tiniest details of life he reminds you of his presence. "Here!" he pipes up. "I'm very here!"

In today's verse, the term refuge calls to mind the walled cities of biblical times, which stood strong against enemy armies. When invaders approached, the farmers and villagers would flee to the cities for safety. Behind those walls of stone they could relax again.

God has that kind of strength. When we face opposition we can run to the Lord for help. Like a walled city, he protects us with his incomparable power.

But there were also cities in Israel that were designated cities of refuge. If, say, you killed someone accidentally, the victim's family could take vengeance and kill you—unless you ran to one of these cities. There you'd be assured a fair trial before the high priest.

That's another wonderful picture of God's protection. We can run to him for understanding, for mercy, even when we've done something wrong. He protects us from spiritual destruction, offering us forgiveness and new life.

What do you need help with? Do you have enemies slandering you, using you, mistreating you? Are you feeling spiritually tempted these days? Is your attitude being dragged down into depression, self-loathing, complacency, or discontent? Run to the Lord for help, and in an instant he will be "very here."

※ ※ ※ ※

WHAT A FRIEND WE HAVE IN JESUS

What a friend we have in Jesus,
all our sins and griefs to bear!
What a privilege to carry
ev'rything to God in prayer!
O what peace we often forfeit,
O what needless pain we bear,
all because we do not carry
ev'rything to God in prayer.

Have we trials and temptations?
Is there trouble anywhere?
We should never be discouraged—
take it to the Lord in prayer!
Can we find a friend so faithful,
who will all our sorrows share?
Jesus knows our ev'ry weakness—
take it to the Lord in prayer!

Are we weak and heavy laden,
cumbered with a load of care?

Precious Savior, still our refuge—
take it to the Lord in prayer!
Do your friends despise, forsake you?
Take it to the Lord in prayer!
In his arms he'll take and shield you—
you will find a solace there.

JOSEPH SCRIVEN

BE STILL, MY SOUL: THE LORD IS ON YOUR SIDE!

Be still, my soul: the Lord is on your side!
Bear patiently the cross of grief or pain;
leave to your God to order and provide—
in ev'ry change he faithful will remain.
Be still, my soul: your best, your heav'nly friend
    through thorny ways leads to a joyful end.

Be still, my soul: your God will undertake
to guide the future as he has the past;
your hope, your confidence let nothing shake—
all now mysterious shall be bright at last.
Be still, my soul: the waves and winds still know
his voice who ruled them while he dwelt below.

KATHARINA VON SCHLEGEL
TRANSLATED BY JANE BORTHWICK

JUST A THOUGHT

*God is bigger than any problem
you have. Whoever is opposing
you is a weakling compared to
God. Why not tap into God's
supply of strength? Why focus
on your problem when God is
so much more interesting?*

*The sun does not rise because of
the rotation of the earth. The
sun rises because God says to
it, "Get up!"*

G. K. CHESTERTON

A SPIRITUAL TREASURE

When you pass through the waters, I will be with you;
and through the rivers, they shall not overwhelm you;
when you walk through fire you shall not be burned,
and the flame shall not consume you.

ISAIAH 43:2

THESE WORDS WERE FIRST SPOKEN to the people of Israel, who were going through a period of difficulty. They are words of hope, courage, and strength. The prophet calls to mind the great Exodus from Egypt, when God led the people from slavery to freedom through the parted Red Sea. The prophet reminds the people of what God did in the past and promises that God will again rescue the people with a mighty arm. Whatever difficulty they are facing, God will be with them.

These words are still a source of strength in our world. During the Civil Rights movement in the 1960s marchers faced water cannons and burning crosses. Sometimes during protest marches angry city officials would open the fire hydrants and disperse the marchers with strong blasts from fire hoses. Still the marchers remained nonviolent and persisted in their walk for justice. Cross burnings were fiery signs accompanied often by violence and threats intended to scare off African Americans from living anywhere but the "other side of the tracks." Yet, the people took courage from these words in Isaiah and continued to fight on for better housing and better schools. God stands with people to be their strength in the struggle for justice.

These words can also be a comfort and strength to people going through a difficult time. One woman experienced the pain of losing a child at birth and soon internalized that hurt into a deep depression. Week after week she would come to see me, and we found hope walking on the beach, recalling God's blessings in the past, and reciting these words from Isaiah. She needed to hear that she would not be overwhelmed with grief, that she would not be left alone by God or by those close to her. Those are words that we all need to hear, for life can be pretty overwhelming and often times lonely.

My desk can get pretty messy, and the piles can threaten to take over. The amount of information in the world is staggering, and, according to one report, information now doubles every seven years. There is no way to keep up with the volume of information, no way I am ever going to read everything that comes across my desk. There are days when I (and I am sure many others feel the same way) feel so overwhelmed, I feel like I'm drowning. Work, family, and personal responsibilities can mount up and threaten to sink us.

Isaiah gives us a word of strength in a sea of paperwork. I am learning not to read every piece of mail that comes. I am learning to prioritize. I am learning to take time off so I can remember that God walks with me and helps me know what is really important.

Isaiah 43:2 is a good passage to print on a piece of paper and post in our office or in our home so we don't forget that our strength comes from the Lord.

I am learning the power of affirmations, words that I say to myself in the face of so much negativity. The chief affirmation is found in this Psalm: "I will be with you." I don't face the world alone. I am also strengthened by, "they shall not overwhelm you . . . you shall not be burned, and the flame shall not consume you." God limits the effects of the trouble that comes my way.

In so many ways, Psalm 43 is a spiritual treasure, a wise companion for our journey.

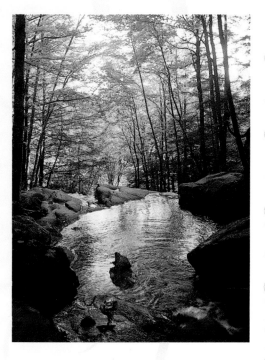

❋ ❋ ❋ ❋

How Firm a Foundation

How firm a foundation, you saints of the Lord,
is laid for your faith in his excellent Word!
What more can he say than to you he has said,
to you who for refuge to Jesus have fled?

When through the deep waters I call you to go,
the rivers of sorrow shall not overflow;
for I will be with you in trouble to bless,
and sanctify to thee thy deepest distress.

When through fiery trials your pathways shall lie,
my grace all sufficient shall be your supply;
the flame shall not hurt you; I only design
your dross to consume and your gold to refine.

JOHN RIPPON

A MIGHTY FORTRESS

Incline your ear to me; rescue me speedily.
Be a rock of refuge for me, a strong fortress to save me.

PSALM 31:2

THE BATTLE HYMN of the Reformation, as it is sometimes called, was written by the son of a copper miner. After the young man finished college in 1505, he became a preacher instead of a lawyer, as his father had intended. He didn't do what a lot of other people wanted him to do either, especially Pope Leo X.

After being ordained a priest, he visited Rome in 1510 and was disillusioned by what he saw as corruption by some the church's leaders.

The young priest returned to the university where he was teaching in Wittenburg, Germany, and there he nailed 95 statements to the door, protesting that no one, not even the Pope, had the power to forgive sins. The man, of course, was Martin Luther, and the song was "A Mighty Fortress Is Our God."

Luther knew something about fortresses. His teachings were so controversial that the Emperor convened a special council at Worms, calling for Luther to recant, which he would not do. So Luther was banned from the empire, but he was then taken under the custody and protection of a nobleman in Wartburg who staged a "kidnaping" to protect Luther from his enemies.

It was there, at the fortress in Wartburg, that Luther translated the Bible into German. This was the first translation to allow ordinary people access to Scripture. And it was there, too, that he probably received the inspiration for this powerful hymn about God's protection.

Luther's music was simple and folklike, much like the man himself. "Music is an outstanding gift of God," wrote Luther. "I would not want to give up my slight knowledge of music for a great consideration." Altogether he wrote 37 hymns.

In some ways, Luther's music was as great a gift as his theology, and in some ways he combined the two. "A Mighty Fortress Is Our God" is based on Psalm 46, which begins "God is our refuge and strength, an ever-present help in trouble," and it ends with "The God of Jacob is our fortress."

Both David's psalms and Luther's song continue to encourage us because our God is still a mighty fortress.

A MIGHTY FORTRESS IS OUR GOD

A mighty fortress is our God,
a bulwark never failing;
our helper he amid the flood
of mortal ills prevailing.
For still our ancient foe
Doth seek to work us woe—
his craft and pow'r are great,
and, armed with cruel hate,
on earth is not his equal.

Did we in our own strength confide,
our striving would be losing,
were not the right one on our side,
the one of God's own choosing.
You ask who that may be?
Christ Jesus, it is he—
Lord Sabaoth his name,
from age to age the same,
and he must win the battle.

MARTIN LUTHER

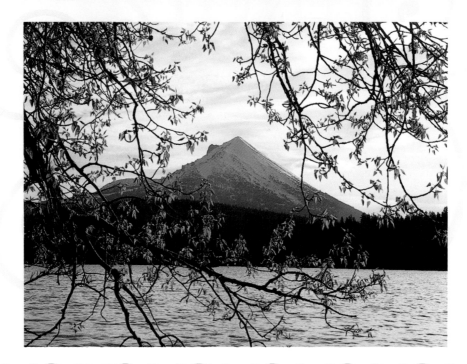

THE TIME OF TROUBLE

The salvation of the righteous is from the Lord;
he is their refuge in time of trouble.

PSALM 37:39

STEVEN SPIELBERG'S masterpiece movie, *Schindler's List*, shows people "in time of trouble" turning to an unlikely refuge. In Germany in the 1930s and 1940s Jews were rounded up and sent to concentration camps for no other "crime" than being Jewish. Schindler was a ruthless businessman who had dealings with the German government, but he managed to protect a number of Jews by hiring them and listing them as essential workers. In a very real way he provided "salvation" for them. From his position of economic strength he offered refuge, and his Jewish employees were able to outlast their Nazi tormentors.

If the psalmist were a filmmaker, Psalm 37 might be similar to *Schindler's List*. The problem is simple: The bad guys have all the power. They're getting away with murder, literally, while good people are victimized. It's not fair! It's not right! It's not supposed to work this way!

That's a common complaint in the psalms, and this one starts with assurances for the victims: "Do not fret because of the wicked; do not be envious of wrong-doers, for they will soon fade like the grass" (Psalm 37:1–2). Evil people may be living it up now, but their success is temporary. "Their day is coming," says verse 13. It is the meek who will inherit the earth (see verse 11 and Matthew 5:5).

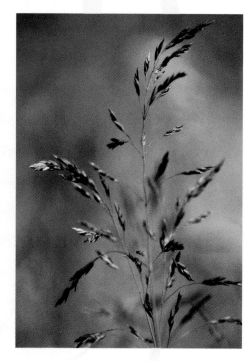

It's always a temptation for the "righteous"—those who seek to please God—to take matters into their own hands. They might adopt some practices of the wicked in order to even the score. But this psalm warns against that.

A high school basketball team was getting frustrated when they played a stronger, more physical team. The bumps and shoves from the opposition were throwing them off their well-drilled plays, and the referees weren't calling all the fouls. "Stay on your game," the coach kept saying. "Don't play their way."

The team was falling 10, 12, 15 points behind, but the coach remained committed to their system. He even yanked one player who started pushing the opponents back. "Be patient," he said. "It will even out."

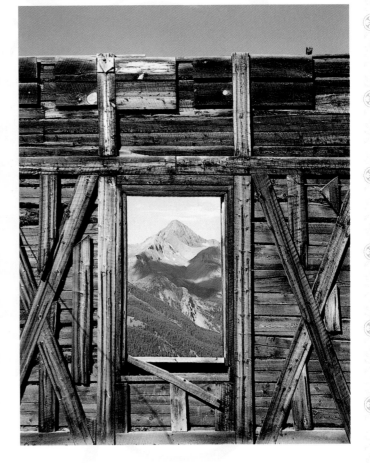

In the fourth quarter the opposing team had to rest some players who were in danger of fouling out. The patient team started to cut into the lead, running their plays methodically, just as they had practiced. In the final minute, one of the opposing players tried to pick a fight and got called for a technical foul. The resulting points put the patient team ahead for good.

That's the psalmist's advice to the faithful: Stay on your game. "Commit your way to the Lord; trust in him, and he will act" (Psalm 37:5). It isn't over until it's over.

God shelters his people in the short term and rewards them in the long term. Like a celestial Schindler, he offers protection from the evil devices of enemies. He uses his strength as a refuge for those who trust him.

Does that mean bad things will never happen to believers? No. In fact, the Bible acknowledges that we will have "times of trouble." But they are just times, temporary moments of difficulty within an eternity of joy. God has all the time in the world (and then some) to grant our desires. Within this earthly life, he often provides amazing strength and support to his followers. He works miracles to save us from some of our current problems. But we can bank on the fact that our long-term safety is guaranteed. Our salvation is not only from the Lord; it's in the Lord. He gives us eternal refuge as we hide ourselves in him.

The night is given us to take breath, to pray, to drink deep at the fountain of power. The day, to use the strength which has been given us, to go forth to work with it till the evening.

FLORENCE NIGHTINGALE

STRENGTH AND SHIELD

*The Lord is my strength and my shield; in him my heart trusts;
so I am helped, and my heart exults, and with my song I give
thanks to him. The Lord is the strength of his people; he is the
saving refuge of his anointed. O save your people, and bless
your heritage; be their shepherd, and carry them forever.*

PSALM 28:7–9

WHEN MY SON was younger, he enjoyed tales about King Arthur and the knights of the round table. This enduring English story is filled with heroes and battles, romance and conquests. I believe my son liked the battles best; he would often fashion a sword and shield. The sword would be for offense, striking a blow at the invisible enemy, and the shield was for defense against the thrusts of the attacker. The psalmist uses the same kind of imagery, only God becomes both the offensive strength and the defensive shield.

The psalmist probably doesn't see God with a sword, but the author is in trouble and believes that

God will come to give strong assistance. God will be the strength needed to battle the wicked, those "who are workers of evil, who speak peace with their neighbors, while mischief is in their hearts" (verse 3). God will also be a shield to protect the author from harm. John Wesley, the founder of Methodism, would encourage his followers to do good,

fight injustice, and refrain from doing evil. There was wisdom in his counsel, for sometimes we need to be active in doing good and fighting injustice, and at other times the best we can do is hold up our shield to resist evil. With God as strength and shield we are ready to initiate battle or to resist the advances of the enemy.

These verses of thanksgiving and trust come at the end of the plea for help. The psalmist is confident that God will come; "he has heard the sound of my pleadings" (Psalm 28:6). The psalmist takes courage from the coming of God and states boldly, "I am helped." God helps us face the ordinary hardships of life, whether they be at home, at work, or at school. It is no surprise, then, that the psalmist wants to sing, to praise God with songs of thanksgiving. You might want to remember a time when God was a source of strength and great help to you and write your own song of thanksgiving.

The psalmist is not finished. Not only does God work with individuals, but God is also actively involved in saving the nation. God is the strength of the poet and of the whole community.

In the United States we observe a National Day of Prayer in May. It is to be a reminder that a strong nation knows there is a greater power. It is also a reminder that great nations learn how to take care of the poor, the least, and the forgotten. Our strength as a nation comes not from armaments but from our compassion for the needy, for the hungry, for children, and for the elderly—for taking care of those who are least able to help themselves. "The Lord is the strength of his people," and God's name is love. We do not rely on our own strength, but we harness our capacities to the direction of God, who is full of kindness and compassion.

God promises to be with us as individuals and as a nation. God wants to be our strength and shield, longer

lasting than Camelot, more compassionate than King
Arthur, and more inclusive than the knights of the
round table.

❀   ❀   ❀   ❀

O GOD, OUR HELP IN AGES PAST

O God, our help in ages past,
our hope for years to come,
our shelter from the stormy blast,
and our eternal home!

Under the shadow of your throne
your saints have dwelt secure;
sufficient is your arm alone,
and our defense is sure.

O God, our help in ages past,
our hope for years to come,
be now our guide while life shall last,
and our eternal home.

ISAAC WATTS

❀   ❀   ❀   ❀

Nothing is so strong as gentleness,
nothing so gentle as real strength.

ST. FRANCIS DE SALES

A HIDING PLACE

*I love you, O Lord, my strength. The Lord is my rock, my fortress,
and my deliverer, my God, my rock in whom I take refuge, my
shield, and the horn of my salvation, my stronghold.*
PSALM 18:1–2

WHEN I WAS FIVE, my family moved from the flat, sandy shores of south Florida to the rocky ridges of east Tennessee. There were a lot of adjustments to be made. The first time it snowed I ran outside barefoot—I had no idea what was coming from the skies.

My dad was in school, studying for the ministry, and he became the pastor of a small church tucked away on the side of Signal Mountain. We lived in Chattanooga, and our days were filled with heavy traffic and dense smog. But on the weekends we went up to the church, both Saturday and Sunday. These mountain people were different, and they ate strange foods—although I'm sure they thought the same thing about us.

What I really enjoyed was the mountain itself. I spent hours and hours playing in and around huge rocks, some of them as large as houses. There were caves to explore, rocks to climb on, and places to hide from my little sister.

We moved back to Florida when I was ten, but years later I returned to Tennessee. My wife and I were married on that mountain, and later we lived near the little country church. Even then I was drawn to the rocks.

Sometimes I would sit on or beside one rock that was about 10 feet high and 15 feet long, which stood just in front of our house. I would contemplate its immensity and the immensity of the God who made it. It was a safe, secure place.

Others have felt the same way. Augustus Toplady wrote the popular hymn "Rock of Ages" after taking shelter under a huge rock near Somersetshire, England, during a terrible storm.

And a few years ago, when I visited Israel, I imagined King David as a young shepherd boy playing on the rocky ridges of Judea. He later hid from a jealous king in these same caves, and he wrote many psalms that celebrated the strength of those rocks and the God who made them. "The Lord is my rock," he wrote. "My rock in whom I take refuge."

It's easy to understand why.

HIDING IN THEE

O safe to the rock that is higher than I
my soul in its conflicts and sorrows would fly;
so sinful, so weary—thine, thine would I be:
Thou blest "Rock of Ages," I'm hiding in thee.

In the calm of the noontide, in sorrow's lone hour,
in times when temptation's casts o'er me its power,
in the tempests of life, on its wide heaving sea,
thou blest "Rock of Ages," I'm hiding in thee.

How oft in the conflict, when pressed by the foe,
I have fled to my refuge and breathed out my woe;
how often, when trials like sea billows roll,
have I hidden in thee, O thou rock of my soul.

Hiding in thee, hiding in thee,
thou blest "Rock of Ages," I'm hiding in thee.

WILLIAM CUSHING

*Lord,
I'm glad I can hide in you. I'm
glad that you are a strong,
safe place of refuge. Thank you
for being my Rock.
Amen.*

ROCK OF AGES

Rock of ages, cleft for me,
let me hide myself in thee;
let the water and the blood
from thy wounded side which flowed,
be of sin the double cure,
save from wrath and make me pure.

Could my tears forever flow,
could my zeal no longer know,
these for sin could not atone—
thou must save, and thou alone:
In my hand no price I bring,
simply to thy cross I cling.

While I draw this fleeting breath,
when my eyes shall close in death,
when I rise to worlds unknown
and behold thee on thy throne,
Rock of Ages, cleft for me,
let me hide myself in thee.

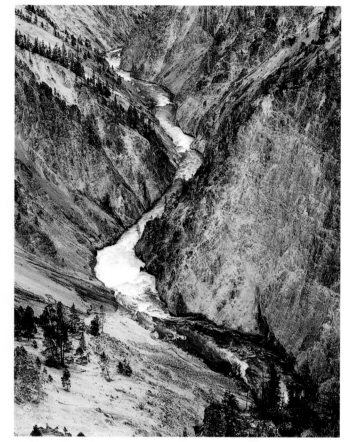

AUGUSTUS TOPLADY

ARE WE THERE YET?

And after you have suffered for a little while, the God of all grace,
who has called you to his eternal glory in Christ, will himself
restore, support, strengthen, and establish you.

1 PETER 5:10

"ARE WE THERE YET?"

What parent doesn't know that plaintive cry? You buckle the kids in the backseat for the ten-hour drive to Grandma's house, and within ten minutes they're travel-weary.

"Are we there yet?"

No, you reply, it'll be a while yet. Let's sing a song. So you sing a song that has a hundred verses; its dippy melody forever etching itself on your brain. You hope it might have lulled the kids to sleep, but no . . .

"Are we there yet?"

No, only nine-and-a-half hours to go. Let's look at license plates.

"Are we there yet?"

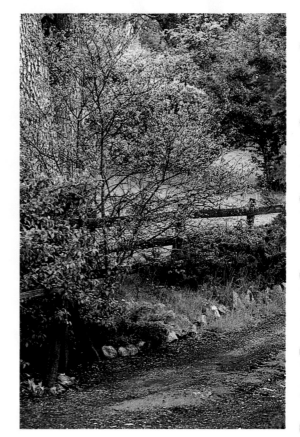

Maybe God feels this way with us sometimes. To him a day is like a thousand years—ten minutes, ten hours, what's the difference? But time drags slowly for us, especially when we're in tough times. God promises that he'll get us out of our troubles in "a little while," and we keep asking, "Are we there yet? Are we? Are we?"

When Peter wrote this verse, Christians were beginning to go through some serious persecution. Peter himself would be crucified in a crackdown ordered by Emperor Nero. After Nero, things eased up for a few decades, until Emperor Domitian wanted to be worshiped as a god and arrested those who refused. So it went for 250 years—suffering, calm, suffering, calm. At times it was brutal—unarmed Christians facing trained gladiators or fierce animals in the arena as the crowds cheered and jeered. You can't blame them for asking, "Are we there yet?"

But today's verse reminds us that God has a plan, and God has a process. He has called his people to "eternal glory." The current sufferings are temporary.

They're painful, to be sure, but they won't last forever. When we reach eternity, the time of turmoil will seem like only "a little while."

And even in the midst of suffering, God does not leave his followers. He is actively restoring, supporting, strengthening, and establishing us. There's a progression here, a process. He picks us up when we're down, holds us up, gives us power to stand, and ultimately enables us to help others.

Have you noticed that? After you recover from a crisis you are better able to help others who are going through that same kind of crisis. God has strengthened you, and now he can use you to strengthen others.

So when others are asking, "Are we there yet?" you can be the one to say, "No, not yet, but we'll get there. God has promised us a wonderful future that will make us forget all about these sufferings. But in the meantime, he gives us the strength we need to get through."

When God wants to move a mountain, he does not take a bar of iron, but he takes a little worm. The fact is, we have too much strength. We are not weak enough. It is not our strength that we want. One ounce of God's strength is worth more than all the world.

DWIGHT L. MOODY

When God contemplates some great work, he begins it by the hand of some poor, weak, human creature, to whom he afterward gives aid, so that the enemies who seek to obstruct it are overcome.

MARTIN LUTHER

GOD PROMISES FORGIVENESS

⊛ ⊛ ⊛ ⊛

BE MERCIFUL, just as your Father is merciful. Do not judge, and you will not be judged; do not condemn, and you will not be condemned. Forgive, and you will be forgiven.

LUKE 6:36–37

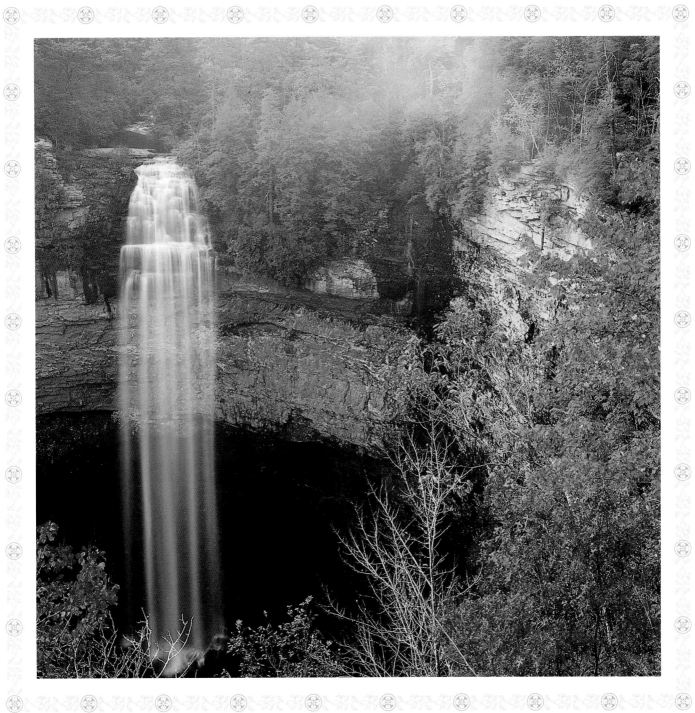

JOURNEY TO FORGIVENESS

What do you think? If a shepherd has a hundred sheep, and one of them has gone astray, does he not leave the ninety-nine on the mountains and go in search of the one that went astray? And if he finds it, truly I tell you, he rejoices over it more than over the ninety-nine that never went astray. So it is not the will of your Father in heaven that one of these little ones should be lost.

MATTHEW 18:12–14

GOD IS SEARCHING for you, longing for you to come home. The love of God is woven so strongly throughout the Gospels. Jesus is forever using stories and illustrations of God's yearning for us.

Imagine you are the missing sheep in this story. You have been separated from the rest of the flock. You may have been hurt in a fall. You may just have wandered off, curious and distracted, and now you are frightened because you do not know the way home. Off in the distance you hear a familiar voice. It is the voice of the shepherd, a voice that calms your fears and gives you hope. The shepherd is coming for you. You are worth the time and effort of the shepherd. You are precious to the shepherd and certainly worth the search. You are found. There is great rejoicing.

It is a common story in the Gospels, a story that the hearers knew was meant for them. They were loved by God, who eagerly sought them and would greatly rejoice if they would come home. It is a story that still touches lives today. It is a story that has our name written around the collar of the lost sheep.

Marge was grieving over the loss of her husband of 35 years. For the first time in her life, she was alone and somewhat isolated because she had always depended on her husband to drive. A friend invited her to church, and she found a community that knew how to grieve and how to dance. She found others who had also lost husbands, and  together they began to meet at the church for support. She said it was like being lost and then finding a new home where the healing could take place.

An issue for most in the group was forgiveness. Some were having trouble forgiving themselves. They had said or done things they wish they had not done. They wished they had made other choices about the care of their loved ones. They wished they had been stronger and not given up hope. They were sorry they had not taken that put-off special trip or had retired earlier. They were having a hard time forgiving themselves for what they had and had not done.

Others in the group were having a hard time forgiving their partners for dying. They were angry about being left alone and angry that their partners did not take better care of themselves or had ignored danger signs. Their grief was complicated by their anger—and their shame over that anger.

God seeks us out, whenever we are lost, and one of the lost places is the tricky thornbush of forgiveness. God wants us to experience forgiveness, wants to bring us back to the joyous party, but we resist or wander off, stuck in our own bad mood.

Forgiveness is a process, a journey that often begins slowly. Forgiveness involves remembering. Some small offenses can be forgotten or overlooked, but for persistent or large wounds it is necessary, though often painful, to remember. The wound or trouble needs to be acknowledged in order for the healing to begin. Some find it helpful to retrieve some happier moments of the relationship before reviewing the hurt. Let yourself feel the pain and then review the consequences. What are your losses? What would you like to recover?

A second part of the journey to forgiveness is to trust your ability to understand, to pray for the grace of insight. Look within yourself, and see the part you may have played in the troubling event. Look inside the other person, and see if there was some wound they were carrying. Do not look for excuses or to assign blame; seek only to understand.

The hardest part of forgiveness is deciding to forgive. It does not make sense, for we often want to settle a score or punish ourselves. There are, of course, some times when courts or the government need to intervene. But when reconciliation is not possible, one still needs to deal with the inner dynamics. Forgiveness is something we do for ourselves in order to move on. Holding on to resentments or anger traps us in the past. Forgiving frees us from dwelling in the troubled past.

Are you willing to let go of what happened, let go of your feelings associated with the hurt?

Through the journey, invite God to walk with you. God does not desire one of the sheep to be lost to anger, resentment, or worry. God wants to bring you out from the thorny quagmire of unforgiven hurts. God wants you to come home.

God loves to forgive. It is the one thing he yearns to do, aches to do, rushes to do. At the very heart of the universe is God's desire to give and to forgive.

RICHARD FOSTER, *PRAYER: FINDING THE HEART'S TRUE HOME*

REJOICE WITH ME

Just so, I tell you, there is joy in the presence
of the angels of God over one sinner who repents.

LUKE 15:10

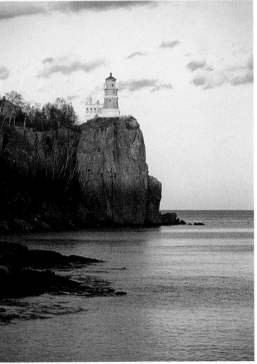

I SPEND A LOT of time looking for things that are lost: lost keys, lost glasses, lost papers—especially lost papers. I'm a teacher, and I'm always making copies of interesting articles, stacking them in piles, and then placing them in files. Soon I have piles of files.

Then, when something comes up in class or in a project, I think, "Oh, I read something about that. Now let's see, where did I put that article . . ."

If it is important enough, I start sorting through things, and usually I can find what I need. Often I can do this in just minutes, because the things I remember best are closest to the top of one pile. And if I can't find it easily, I move on, anticipating the day when I will have all this organized. My wife is pretty certain such a day will never come, but she is the kind of person who always puts her glasses in the same place.

Sometimes, however, I need a specific piece of information, and I will spend days looking for it. I realize this is not a good use of my time. But what I am looking for is often the piece I need to finish an article or make a case for a new program at school.

Often, when Katie calls to ask what I'm doing, I have to tell her, "I'm looking for the article I need." She is a nice person, so she doesn't say, "If you'd figure out how to keep a filing system, you wouldn't be wasting your life like this." Instead, she says, "I'll pray that you will find it," and she does.

Later, when I find what I need, I call her back, and she's glad for me. But she's never as glad as I am. That's because when I lose something important, it becomes even more important to me. And the more important it is, the happier I am when I find it.

Jesus knew this was true, and he told his disciples about a woman who had ten silver coins, but she lost one. There were few windows back then, and houses were dark. But the woman lit a lantern, and she swept the whole house looking for her lost coin.

These were silver coins, and it would take her a while to save enough to replace one. And they may also have had sentimental value, as part of her dowry, perhaps. If so, she may have worn all ten coins on a necklace, and her friends would have noticed immediately that one was missing.

So she searched everywhere, and when she found it, she called her friends and neighbors together. Then she had a party. "Rejoice with me," she said. "I have found the coin that I had lost." "Just so," Jesus said, "There is joy in the presence of the angels of God over one sinner who repents."

Jesus told this story when the pharisees accused him of eating with sinners. He told two other stories, too. He told about a shepherd who had 99 sheep safe in the fold, but he went out to find a missing one. And he told about a son who left home and squandered his fortune. The son returned to his father, who had missed him, and the father "killed the fatted calf" when he returned. In every case, there was rejoicing when the lost thing was found.

Lord,
When I turn to you and trust
you, you are very glad.
Make me glad, too, as I learn
to share your joy in finding
what you lost.
Amen

God has lost something, too, and Jesus said he feels the same way when he finds it. He is willing to go to great extremes to find the sinners the pharisees despised. When God finds one, there is a party in heaven. The angels rejoice, and their joy is God's joy. In fact, God doesn't just smile. He sings. The prophet Zephaniah says "The Lord, your God, is in your midst, a warrior who gives victory; he will rejoice over you with gladness, he will renew you in his love; he will exult over you with loud singing" (Zephaniah 3:17).

That's quite a celebration, and it must be quite a song.

EXCUSES, EXCUSES

Then Jesus said, "Father, forgive them;
for they do not know what they are doing."

LUKE 23:34

IGNORANCE IS BLISS, they say. But not always
for the other person. When another driver
cuts you off on the highway, it probably
doesn't matter to you whether he knew
what he was doing. You're upset, and rightly so.

When a CEO bungles the company's business plan
so badly that there are layoffs—and you lose your job
while he gets a golden parachute—his ignorance does
not make you feel any better.

When the sales clerk at the department store ignores
you for five minutes while chatting with a friend, then
hits the wrong key and has to wait for a supervisor to
correct it, you don't really care that it's her first day on
the job. You've been mistreated! You should not have
had to wait!

When the person in front of you in the "10 Items or
Less" checkout line unloads 23 (count 'em) things from
her cart and haggles over each price, you could chalk it

up to a reading deficiency or a math deficiency, but it doesn't change the fact that you've been sinned against. Your quick trip to the market is lasting longer than *War and Peace!*

Today's verse is a statement made by Jesus, not in a checkout line or on a superhighway, but on a cross. He wasn't being inconvenienced; he was being killed. And still he reached out with a kindness we often lack, forgiving the ones who pounded the nails into his hands.

He offers the same forgiveness to us when we disappoint him, when we disobey him, when we pretend we don't know him. No sin is too great for his grace. Whatever you've done, he will forgive you.

But what was this about: "They do not know what they are doing"? Of course they knew! The Roman soldiers were experts at killing criminals, making it as painful as possible. The political and religious leaders who arranged Jesus' arrest, conviction, and sentencing knew exactly what they were doing. They wanted to get rid of Jesus, and they did. The passersby who mocked him had no excuses, either. Some of them even quoted his own words as they taunted him to come down from the cross. Make no mistake: This sin was wide-eyed and deliberate. Just like many of the sins we commit.

So what was Jesus talking about?

In any sin there's an element of ignorance. Maybe the soldiers didn't realize they were crucifying the Son of God. Some of the leaders probably thought they were serving God, and that Jesus was an impostor. Many of those who put Jesus on the cross probably never realized how much they were hurting God. If they knew, how could they have done that?

The same is true of our sin. Even our most intentional "I want my own way" sins have an element of ignorance. We may think we know what we're doing, but we don't. We don't realize how much pain we're causing God.

Amazingly, through his pain, God takes pity on us. He sees us as beloved children with a lot to learn. Just as he saw Adam and Eve in the garden, being duped by a snake. If we only knew what joy we were trading for one bite of forbidden fruit, we'd never do it. In his love, he grants us forgiveness. Don't be too ignorant to accept it.

THE KING OF LOVE MY SHEPHERD IS

The King of love my Shepherd is,
whose goodness fails me never;
I nothing lack if I am his
and he is mine forever.

In death's dark vale I fear no ill
with you, dear Lord, beside me;
your rod and staff my comfort still,
and home, rejoicing, brought me.

And so through all the length of days
your goodness fails me never:
Good Shepherd, may I sing
your praise within your house forever.

HENRY W. BAKER

MERCY FOR THE KING

Have mercy on me, O God, according to your steadfast love;
according to your abundant mercy blot out my transgressions.
Wash me thoroughly from my iniquity, and cleanse me from my
sin. . . . Deliver me from bloodshed, O God, O God of my salvation,
and my tongue will sing aloud of your deliverance.

PSALM 51:1–2,14

THE KING WENT WALKING on his penthouse patio, and he saw, across the way, a bathing beauty. He wanted her, and, since he was king, he got her. He also got her pregnant.

This was a problem. After all, it was ancient Israel, a nation that followed God's laws. Adultery was wrong, and the king would be scandalized if this became public.

So he attempted a cover-up. The woman's husband served in the army. That was convenient. Simply call him back from the front lines and grant him a relaxing weekend with his wife. Everyone will think the baby is his. Brilliant!

But the soldier couldn't bear the thought of enjoying his wife's company while his soldiers were suffering on the front lines. He slept at the entrance of the king's palace, foiling the king's careful plot.

And so an ugly story got even uglier. The soldier was sent back to the front, and the general was ordered to abandon him in the heat of the conflict. The soldier would die in battle, a war hero, and the king would graciously take the war widow as his own queen. What a public relations coup! And no one would ever know the real dirt.

Except God, who sent a prophet to tell the king a story. You see, king, this poor man had one lamb that he loved dearly. But a rich man stole that lamb and killed the poor man. The king was enraged that such injustice would go on in his kingdom. He had been a poor shepherd once himself, and he knew how precious a single lamb could be. "Who is that rich man?" he demanded, vowing to make him pay.

You are the man, the prophet replied, and suddenly King David knew the jig was up. He had to come clean about his sin. He confessed publicly, donning the humiliating garb of sackcloth and ashes. And he wrote a prayer of repentance, pleading with God for forgiveness of his sins.

We have it here, Psalm 51, from which these verses are drawn. It's obvious the man feels dirty. He needs to be cleaned. He's like the toddler who has just finger-painted the living room wall—he's caught red-handed and blue-handed and yellow-handed. There's no hiding the crime. He can only hope his forgiving Father will sweep him up in his arms and wash him.

No excuses. No alibis. No getting off on a technicality. He did wrong, and he knows it. He can only throw himself at the mercy of the court. Fortunately for us, the Judge has plenty of mercy. Salvation is his middle name.

Do you have some sin lurking in the corners of your conscience? Maybe you've hid it successfully from everyone else, but God knows. You can't explain it, excuse it, defend it, amend it. You're guilty as sin.

Well, it's time to come clean. God promises forgiveness to those who repent. Through the blood of Christ, he will blot out your transgression and wash you thoroughly.

JUST A THOUGHT

Victor Hugo's classic tale *Les Miserables* testifies to the power of forgiveness. Early in the story, Jean Valjean is forgiven for stealing some silver from the bishop, and he's given a chance to start a new life. He never forgets it, as he grows into an influential businessman. Through the rest of his life he displays a giving, forgiving spirit.

It's a fact: Forgiven people forgive others. Jesus even put this principle in the Lord's Prayer—"Forgive us our trespasses, as we forgive those who trespass against us." Receive the forgiveness God grants you, and then extend it to others.

Lord, I confess to you,
 sadly, my sin;
all I am, I tell to you,
 all I have been.
Purge all my sin away,
wash clean my soul
 this day;
Lord, make me clean.

Then all is peace and
 light this soul within;
thus shall I walk with you,
 loved though unseen.
Leaning on you, my God,
guided along the road,
nothing between!
   HORATIUS BONAR

A NIGHT OF BLESSING

Bless the Lord, O my soul, and do not forget all his benefits—who forgives all your iniquity, who heals all your diseases.

PSALM 103:2–3

TWO OF HUMANITY'S greatest concerns are addressed in these wonderful verses from this powerful psalm of thanksgiving—sin and illness. God is involved in forgiving our mistakes, our sins, our errors. God is actively working to heal our wounds, our illnesses, our diseases. The poet reminds us not to forget the many ways God is touching our lives, bringing us many benefits. Above all, do not forget to thank God for these kindnesses.

I experienced the weaving of blessing and forgiveness in a powerful way at a men's retreat. One evening we were given a strip of red tape and instructed to go off by ourselves and reflect on the wounds that we as men had experienced. They could be physical or emotional wounds we had received. As we remembered the wounds, we were to put a piece of red tape on the spot of the wound. As we gathered back in the candlelit room, we were divided into groups of ten and invited to sit on the floor. Each man was decorated with red pieces of tape. All of us were carrying wounds from life. The leaders invited us to think of words that we wished we had heard from our fathers when we were born, words of blessing and encouragement. We were then instructed to go around the circle and whisper those words to each man.

In the darkened room, sitting there conscious of my past, my wounds, I heard nine blessings whispered to me. "I am glad you are here. May you be filled with joy and courage." "I love you and pray you will follow your dreams." "I am here for you. I will take time with you." It was an incredibly healing night to receive the blessings and to be able to give my blessing to the others. There were tears shed in that small group. And when the last person finished giving his blessing, we all just sat there, not wanting to move or let go of the moment. We took off the red pieces of tape and felt whole, forgiven, and healed.

Bless the Lord, O my Soul, and
all that is within me,
bless his holy name.
PSALM 103:1

I learned a lot about the importance of giving blessings that night. I learned a lot about healing. I learned about the importance of rituals that let us acknowledge the past and open us to receiving forgiveness or healing. I remembered these verses from Psalm 103 and hoped I would not forget the way that God works through others to bring about forgiveness and healing.

ONE THERE IS, ABOVE ALL OTHERS

One there is, above all others,
well deserves the name of Friend;
his is love beyond a mother's,
costly, free, and knows no end;
they who once his kindness prove
find it everlasting love.

Oh, for grace our hearts to soften!
Teach us, Lord, at length to love!
We, alas, forget too often
what a Friend we have above:
but when home our souls are brought
we will love you as we ought.

JOHN NEWTON

A GOD OF HUGS

The Lord is merciful and gracious, slow to anger and abounding in steadfast love. He will not always accuse, nor will he keep his anger forever. He does not deal with us according to our sins, nor repay us according to our iniquities. For as the heavens are high above the earth, so great is his steadfast love toward those who fear him; as far as the east is from the west, so far he removes our transgressions from us.

PSALM 103:8–12

"THE LORD IS MERCIFUL and gracious, slow to anger and abounding in steadfast love." This sentence, or some variation of it, was very important to the Hebrews. In fact, it is quoted or referred to nine times in the Old Testament.

Hezekiah quoted it when Jerusalem was under siege. Nehemiah quoted it when they rebuilt the temple. Joel quoted it when he called the people back to God. The psalmist quoted it at least four times. Jonah even quoted it as a reason not to obey God when he was called to preach to his enemies in Nineveh. "That is why I fled to Tarshish," he said. "I knew that you are a gracious God and merciful, slow to anger, and abounding in steadfast love, and ready to relent from punishing."

It is not difficult to understand why these words were so important to the Hebrews, however. It was God's own way of describing himself when he appeared to Moses and gave him the law written on tablets of stone for the second time.

Think for a moment about what was happening. God speaks from Mount Sinai in a cloud with lightning and thunder and gives the children of Israel the Ten Commandments. Then Moses goes up into the mountains and gets a copy carved in stone.

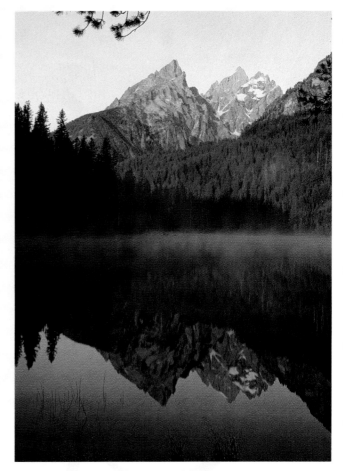

He spends 40 days up there, getting instructions about how to build and run the tabernacle, and when he comes down, the Israelites have built a golden calf and are dancing around it naked—even though God had just delivered them from slavery in Egypt and said aloud that they were not to build idols.

So Moses throws down the tablets and breaks them, and then he gets a few Levites to carve up some of the rebels with swords to bring some order back to the place. Then he climbs back up the mountain to apologize.

We can imagine that he was a little nervous. He was a failure. The people were failures. And yet the first thing God says is, "I am the Lord, a God merciful and gracious, slow to anger, and abounding in steadfast love and faithfulness."

The children of Israel were surrounded by people who sacrificed their children to idols, people who saw their gods as selfish and demanding and capricious. No wonder this statement had such an impact on their national consciousness.

The word translated "gracious" came from a Hebrew root that means "to incline oneself," literally to bow or bend, especially toward an inferior. This is an incredible word picture. In the middle of the people's weakness and failings, God says, "I am the God who inclines himself toward you, who bows down to meet you on your level."

And the word translated "merciful" comes from a root that means "to fondle," and it is translated elsewhere as a woman's womb. It means to enclose, to provide every need, to hold. So what God was saying is

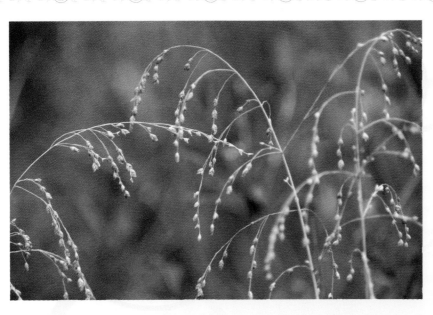

"I am the Lord, the God who looks you in the eye and wants to give you a hug."

Certainly, "He does not deal with us according to our sins, nor repay us according to our iniquities," for "as the heavens are high above the earth, so great is his steadfast love toward those who fear him."

The psalmist who wrote these words found comfort in the God of hugs—and so should we.

❋   ❋   ❋   ❋

Lord,
I'm glad you are merciful and gracious. Today I'm resting in your
steadfast love, and in your hugs.
Amen

God Promises to Hear Our Prayers

I LOVE THE LORD, because he has heard my voice and my supplications. Because he inclined his ear to me, therefore I will call on him as long as I live.

PSALM 116:1–2

ASK, SEARCH, AND KNOCK

Ask, and it will be given you; search, and you will find; knock, and the door will be opened for you. For everyone who asks receives, and everyone who searches finds, and for everyone who knocks, the door will be opened. Is there anyone among you who, if your child asks for bread, will give a stone? Or if your child asks for a fish, will give a snake? If you then, who are evil, know how to give good gifts to your children, how much more will your Father in heaven give good things to those who ask him!

MATTHEW 7:7–11

HAD JUST RETURNED from a conference and was walking to claim my baggage when I noticed an older woman ahead of me, walking slowly and with some difficulty. Just as I noticed her, the young couple who had been sitting next to me on the airplane came abreast of her and asked if they could help. The young man offered to carry her bag, but she declined and instead moved between the couple and took hold of the young woman's arm for support. Slowly, with the older woman voicing her thanks, the three headed to the baggage return.

After retrieving my bags, I boarded a bus to go to the parking lot. Another young couple got on the bus at the next stop. I heard them remark about some roses

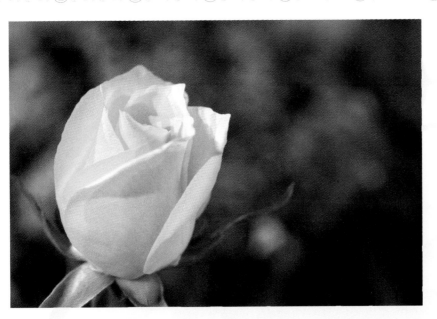

that an older woman sitting near them was holding. The conversation continued in another language, and I did not pay much attention. Then I heard "gracias," and I looked up to see that the older woman had given two beautiful garden roses to the young woman.

I thought if these people, strangers to me and to one another, can show such kindness to each other, imagine the incredible, overflowing, loving intention of God.

Jesus is using graphic images, ordinary experiences to contrast human generosity with divine generosity. If humans can give good gifts, show genuine kindness, care for their youngest, imagine how much more God will care for you. What we experience of kindness in our families and communities is but a foretaste of the great compassion of God, who hears us when we pray and is ready to respond to our needs.

St. Augustine once said, "Our hearts are restless until they find their rest in God." God has put a restlessness in us that keeps us searching, asking, and knocking. People are hungry for meaning in life, for something that lasts longer than the joy of the latest purchase or the most recent success. God is ready to hear our stories and open the door to a deeper relationship.

Asking is most often a verbal activity. We ask a question for information or direction. In our address to God, we ask for guidance, for help. We go to the one who can answer the difficult questions of life, who can show us love, acceptance, and forgiveness. God welcomes our questions, is eager for our interest.

Searching implies some movement and an awareness that something is lost or missing. If God has placed a hunger in our soul, a restlessness in our spirit, then we all are on a quest for the divine. This is not some search for an object, career, or feeling. It is a search for home, for the place where we dwell with our loving Creator.

God welcomes our search and promises that we will find our home in God.

Knocking at a door means we wish to enter another room or place. There is somewhere else we wish to go or explore. God is waiting for our knock and is ready to open the door to a life of meaning, joy, and forgiveness.

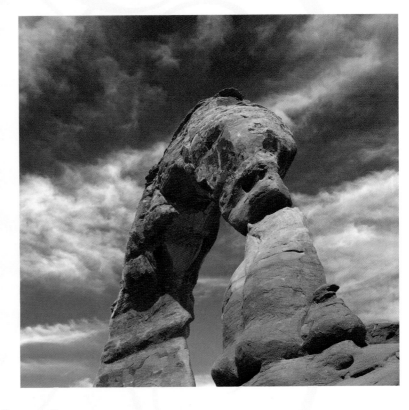

Asking, searching, and knocking are wonderful images that beckon us to move toward God. God is ready and waiting for our inquiry. God put the very desire and hunger in our hearts and promises to hear our prayers, meet our searching, and open the door.

Our confidence in the power of prayer is rooted in the promise that God is continually working for good in the midst of ambiguous situations and that God's purposes will prevail in the end.

MARJORIE THOMPSON,
SOUL FEAST, AN INVITATION TO THE CHRISTIAN SPIRITUAL LIFE

SHARE A PRAYER

Again, truly I tell you, if two of you agree on earth about any-
thing you ask, it will be done for you by my Father in heaven. For
where two or three are gathered in my name, I am there among them.
MATTHEW 18:19–20

SHORTLY AFTER Dallas Seminary was founded in 1924, the new school was threatened with bankruptcy. The creditors were going to foreclose, and on the morning of the foreclosure the founders met in the president's office to pray together for God's help in their time of need.

Dr. Harry Ironsides was well known for his short and candid prayers. Characteristically, he simply prayed, "Lord, we know you own the cattle on a thousand hills. Please sell some of them, and send us the money."

While they were praying, a man came into the business office. "I just sold two carloads of cattle and have spent the whole morning trying to make a business deal go through," he said. "It's just not working out, and I feel the Lord is compelling me to give this money to the seminary instead. I don't know if you need it or not, but here's the check." Then he left.

The secretary knew the men were praying earnestly about the financial emergency they were facing, so she went to the door of the president's office and knocked timidly. "I think you should see this, sir," she said.

The president took the check out of her hand. It was for the exact amount they needed. "Harry," he said, "God sold the cattle."

This is only one of many remarkable stories that can be and are told about what happens when people pray together. Such stories were common in the early church, when, according to Luke in his letter to Theopolis, "they all joined together constantly in prayer." As the people devoted themselves to the apostles' teachings and to fellowship, to the breaking of bread and to prayer, "everyone was filled with awe, and many wonders and miraculous signs were done by the apostles."

In fact, the stories were so amazing that sometimes the people who were praying didn't even believe the answer. The Bible tells one story about early Christians

ANOTHER PROMISE

Are any among you sick?
They should call for the
elders of the church and
have them pray over
them, and anoint them
with oil in the name of
the Lord. The prayer of
faith will save the sick,
and the Lord will raise
them up.

JAMES, THE BROTHER OF JESUS,
JAMES 5:14–15

who were praying for Peter to be released from prison,
and when the maid came to tell them he was at the
door, they made fun of her.

A similar thing occurred a few years ago when a bar
was being built in a small town that had always been
dry. A group of people in one church were opposed to
the bar, and they called an all-night prayer meeting asking God to stop the project.

Lightning struck the tavern, and it burned to the
ground. The owner of the bar sued the church, claiming
they were responsible. But the church members hired a
lawyer who claimed they weren't responsible. The
judge was amused. "One thing is clear," he said. "The
tavern owner believes in prayer and the Christians don't."

But of course they should, because Jesus made a
remarkable promise. If just two or three people agree on
something (and that's pretty remarkable in itself), his
Father will do it. These could be people gathered in his
name, seeking his will, experiencing his presence—
under these conditions the power of their prayers
would be magnified.

We often think of prayer as very personal and pri-
vate, and sometimes it is. But there is a synergy in

shared prayer, and the whole is often greater than the sum of its parts.

It's remarkable but true.

· · · ·

HANDS OF PRAYER

More things are wrought by prayer

Than this world dreams of, Wherefore, let thy voice

Rise like a fountain for me night and day.

For what are men better than sheep or goats

That nourish a blind life within the brain,

If, knowing God, they lift not hands of prayer

Both for themselves and those who call them friend?

For so the whole round earth is every way

Bound by gold chains about the feet of God.

ALFRED, LORD TENNYSON, *MORT D'ARTHUR*

Lord,
I often pray for others when I
need to pray with others. Show
me the power of shared prayer
as I meet with others in your
name and in your presence.
Amen.

CRAZY LOVE

I sought the Lord, and he answered me,
and delivered me from all my fears.

PSALM 34:4

THE HEBREW TITLE of Psalm 34, "Praise for Deliverance from Trouble," indicates it was written during a dramatic time in David's life. Dramatic in many ways—David was putting on a performance. You see, David was on the run from King Saul. The king was jealous of David's success in fighting the rival Philistines, and he wanted to do away with this young warrior. After scampering through the Judean desert and foothills, David tried hiding where Saul would never look for him—among the Philistines. Eventually, he was recognized as the guy who had slain thousands of their soldiers (including the famous giant Goliath), and so David had to think of something quick.

He pretended to be insane.

He drooled. He scratched at doors like a dog. Who knows what other antics he came up with? But it all worked. When David was brought to the Philistine king, he wasn't imprisoned or executed, just kicked out

of town. King Achish stared at this pitiful creature and came up with one of the great lines of Scripture: "Am I so short of madmen that you have to bring this fellow here to carry on in front of me?" (1 Samuel 21:15, NIV).

Indeed, life was pretty crazy for David in those days. There may have been moments when he himself wondered whether this was just an act or if he really was losing his mind. But through all of it, as Psalm 34 shows us, he clung to the one thing he knew for certain: The Lord cares.

God will either give you what you ask, or something far better.
ROBERT MURRAY MCCHEYNE

You can bet that when he was pawing the palace gates like an animal he was praying—praying like crazy, you might say. "Lord, get me out of this!" Verse 4 mentions his "fears," and we can be sure that the danger was very real, very immediate. One swipe of a Philistine swd and it was curtains for David, no matter how good an actor he was. He needed major intervention for Achish to buy this act. And that's exactly what happened. The Lord heard his prayer and answered it, delivering David from all his fears.

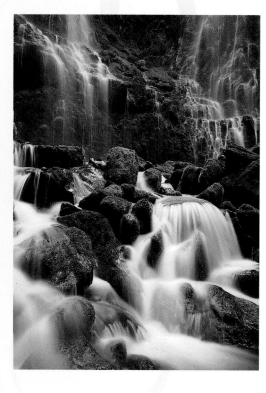

Prayer is a powerful thing, for God has bound and tied himself thereto. None can believe how powerful prayer is, and what it is able to effect, but those who have learned it by experience.
MARTIN LUTHER

When your life drives you bonkers, remember that the Lord cares. When you find yourself paralyzed by fears, call out for help. Bring your requests to God, and he will answer your prayers. And you don't have to put

on an act with him. You don't have to be pretty or
pious, perfect or pompous. David was drooling when he
launched his prayer for help! In whatever condition you
find yourself, present your requests to God, and trust
him to respond in a way that's best for you.

God answers sharp and sudden on some prayers
And thrusts the thing we have prayed for in our face.

ELIZABETH BARRETT BROWNING

*Keep praying, but be thankful that
God's answers are wiser than your prayers.*

WILLIAM CULBERTSON

O magnify the Lord with me;
    with me exalt his name;
when in distress to him I called,
    he to my rescue came.
The hosts of God encamp around
    the dwellings of the just;
deliverance he affords to all
    who in his goodness trust.

NAHUM TATE

LISTEN FIRST, ASK SECOND

Very truly, I tell you, if you ask anything of the Father in my name, he will give it to you. Until now you have not asked for anything in my name. Ask and you will receive, so that your joy may be complete.

JOHN 16:23–24

AS A CHILD, I made up a Christmas list of things I wanted Santa Claus to bring. I dutifully mailed the list to the North Pole (I wonder what the Post Office did with all those letters) and expected Santa Claus to answer my requests. I usually did get a number of toys at Christmas, and in the joy of the day I never remembered to check to see if I received all the things I had asked for. Besides, this was before computers, and I didn't keep a record of the list I sent to Santa.

When I got older and found out that someone other than Santa was reading and responding to the list, I modified my requests. I began to ask for things that were likely or possible for my parents to buy for me. I knew that they would do their best, not only for me but also for my brother and sister. The content of my asking changed as I understood more about the true meaning of Christmas and the generous love of my parents.

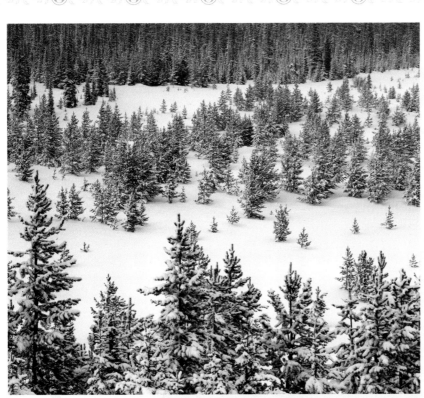

In our prayers of asking, our prayers of petition, there is a similar maturing process. At first we may approach God with a laundry list of things we want for ourselves or for others. The only times we pray are when we want something. We keep talking to God or at God. Such a diet of prayer may turn out to be more frustrating than fulfilling as we begin to notice that God does not seem to be answering. We are not even sure that God hears our requests.

Though God wants us to pray, he longs for a two-way conversation. God desires a deeper relationship. The context for our prayer requests is an ongoing relationship with God, who wants us to listen as well as to speak.

In the development of a child's language skills, listening precedes speaking. Children learn to speak by listening to adults. We learn to address God by developing our ability to listen to God, to encounter God in the wonders of nature, in the poetic verses of the psalms and in the stories of Jesus, in our dreams and in our encounters with people and situations of everyday life. We get to know God as we watch other people pray and live their lives as Christians.

I visited a friend who showed me a diagram of a hand. On each of the fingers was written a type of prayer. The thumb was labeled prayer of adoration. The index finger was prayer of thanksgiving. The middle finger was prayer of confession, and the ring finger was prayer of intercession. The little finger was marked prayer of petition for oneself. I liked the simplicity of the idea. I could be reminded to pray by looking at my hand and moving each finger. I liked a note on the paper that said if the first four kinds (or fingers) of prayer are well developed, than the last and smallest finger of prayer would be in proper perspective. Once again, I had discovered the maturity of prayer. We don't begin with prayers of petition; they flow out of a life of prayer that knows adoration, thanksgiving, confession, and intercession.

As we get to know God better, as we listen as well as speak with God, we will begin to have our prayers of petition shaped by our growing understanding of God's purposes in our lives. We give thanks for the way God has already worked in our lives and in the lives of those dear to us. We give thanks and entrust our prayers to the God who is faithfully and persistently working for good in the world.

Prayer is a participation in willing God's will. While God's ultimate will cannot be thwarted, the strategy God uses to reach that goal may be infinitely variable. The prayers of committed people become part of the cosmic reality God has to work with. God can use them to "tip the balance" and change the shape of distorted reality in our world.

MARJORIE J. THOMPSON, *SOUL FEAST*

A DAD AND HIS LAD

And this is the boldness we have in him, that if we ask anything according to his will, he hears us. And if we know that he hears us in whatever we ask, we know that we have obtained the requests made of him.

1 JOHN 5:14–15

MY WIFE WAS the seventh of ten kids, and she could barely get a word in edgewise. And even if she could, I doubt it would matter much. In some ways her grandparents' strict "children should be seen and not heard" philosophy permeated her Michigan home.

On the other hand, I'm from the South, a fifth generation Floridian, and we were much more laid back. So Katie had reason to think I was spoiled, and she was right. A firstborn son with two much younger sisters, I had—at least when she first met me—the mistaken notion that the planet revolved around my head.

One of the things she found most irritating was my tendency to interrupt people when they were talking, especially older adults. My dad is a pastor. He would be talking to parishioners, and I would walk up to him, ask him a question, and then go on my merry way. I'm not sure which she found more annoying—that I would do it or that he would let me.

But one thing I experienced almost all my life was unrestricted access to my dad. I wasn't allowed to monopolize a conversation, but I could ask a question or make a request at almost any time. And while he may not have been teaching me about good manners, he was teaching me something about prayer.

You see, for years my wife had trouble praying, or at least believing that God was paying any attention to her. But I always felt like he was right there, interested in what I had to say and what I needed.

To some degree, all of us understand who God is and how he works in terms of our own fathers. He is often called Father in the Scriptures, of course, but the New Testament even refers to him with the more familiar Aramaic term *abba*, which means something like "daddy."

I feel fortunate that, at least in this regard, I got the right picture. God is interested in us and what we have to say. The psalmist describes it this way: "On the day I called, you answered me, you increased my strength of soul" (Psalm 138:3).

The Bible promises us access to God's throne, not as a subject, but as a child. It reminds me of a story I heard about Abraham Lincoln. When his young son Tad interrupted a war cabinet meeting in the White House, the president was scolded by one of his generals.

"It's really no bother," Lincoln replied. "This is my son."

I'm glad God feels the same way about me, and about you.

✳   ✳   ✳   ✳

Be Bold

Let us therefore approach the throne of grace with boldness, so that we may receive mercy and find grace to help in time of need.

From the Epistle to the Hebrews

✳   ✳   ✳   ✳

Lord,
I come to you boldly and gladly. Accept me as
your child, and meet my needs.
Amen.

WHEN PEOPLE PRAY

I call upon you, for you will answer me,
O God; incline your ear to me, hear my words.

PSALM 17:6

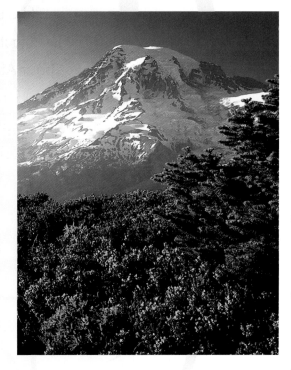

THERE'S NOTHING extraordinary about this handful of Christians who meet Tuesday nights for Bible study and prayer. Marian is new to the Christian faith, drinking it all in with gusto. Janet grew up in a Christian home, but she is just now awakening to the idea of applying her faith to her daily life. Lisa is a leader in the church who has been going through hard times. Arnie has a learning disability, but he goes through life with the mischievous grin of a 12-year-old boy.

And lately they've been learning a lot about prayer.

As they've swapped prayer requests, Arnie has reported that he doesn't get along with his boss. Janet has said she feels used and unappreciated in her job as a nurse. Marian announced months ago that she was

To think
You think
Of me!
How great!

How great
You are,
I think!

I ask;
You give
What
You think
Best.

How great
You are,
I think!

awaiting a liver transplant that could restore her health. Lisa has often shared her frustrations about her elderly mother, who is losing her health and sanity but refuses to move to a nursing home.

Week by week they prayed for one another. And one day Arnie announced he was offered a new job in the same company, with a nicer boss. Soon Janet said she had a whole new attitude at work, and things turned around for her. God was answering their prayers! But weeks turned to months for Marian, and still no liver was available for transplant. And Lisa's mom just kept getting worse.

One Tuesday, Marian was especially distressed. Her doctor had argued with the hospital, and it seemed the transplant wouldn't happen until it was too late for her. The group prayed that the medical people would act with wisdom. The same night Lisa told of an incident with her mother, who had collapsed at home but still refused to move to a nursing facility. The group prayed for healing for the mother and strength for Lisa in the tough decisions she faced.

The next day Marian got a call from the hospital. "The transplant is ready. Get here now!" She did, and the surgery was successful. The day after that, Lisa's mother had to be rushed to the hospital with breathing problems. Within a week she had passed away with a minimum of pain, surrounded by her loved ones.

As Lisa prepared to give the eulogy at her mom's funeral, she called the rest of the group to ask for prayer. "You're batting a thousand so far," she quipped. "It's kind of scary, isn't it?"

Absolutely. The power of God is awesome, and his desire to hear our needs and meet them is astounding. We can't always channel his power in precise ways. Sometimes he surprises us with an unexpected change in circumstance—as he did with Arnie, giving him a new, better job. Sometimes he changes us—as he did with Janet, giving her a positive new attitude. Sometimes we have to wait a long time—like Marian—and just when things look bleakest, he comes through for us. And sometimes he answers in strange ways—taking Lisa's mother to her eternal home rather than a nursing home.

There's nothing extraordinary about this group. You could be a part of it. Week by week they're learning to pray—and to trust that God will answer.

Praise to the Lord; the
    Almighty.
Praise to the Lord
    reigning; above all
    things so wondrously,
Shelt'ring you under his
    wings, and so gently
    sustaining!
Have you not seen all that
    is needful have been
    sent by his gracious
    ordaining?

JOACHIM NEANDER

Between the humble and contrite heart and the majesty of heaven there are no barriers; the only password is prayer.

HOSEA BALLOU

God Hears Our Cries

In my distress I called upon the Lord; to my God
I cried for help. From his temple he heard my voice,
and my cry to him reached his ears.

Psalm 18:6

"Help!"—this is one of the simplest and most poignant of prayers. All of life is not peaches and cream or a box of chocolates. Life can be bruising and painful. Where do we go when things fall apart? Who do we turn to when darkness is all around?

The Jews believed that all of life was related to God. God was creator of all the wonders of the earth, sky, and sea—from the beautiful rose to the soaring eagle to the mighty fish in the sea. As a Jew looked at creation, a prayer of praise and thanksgiving would be spoken. "Blessed are you, Creator of the universe, who brought forth this bread to eat or this new morning." God was praised throughout the day.

The Jews also believed that God was the Lord of history and was intimately involved in their struggle to be freed from slavery in Egypt, to find a new homeland that flowed with milk and honey, and to establish themselves as a nation obedient to God. History sometimes seemed cruel, and instead of happiness there was the bitterness of defeat at the hands of enemy nations.

As the Jews would anguish and lament about their problems, they would take their complaints to God. After all, God was involved in history and would help them. The Book of Psalms is filled with prayers complaining to God about the circumstances of life— whether it be illness, famine, or losing a military battle. When things went wrong, the people prayed to God.

This wonderful verse in Psalm 18 is in the past tense. The prayer of complaint has already been made. Death was already at the door, and God had heard about the problem in a passionate prayer. The prayer turns to thanksgiving. God heard my prayer. My cry reached the very throne of God. My anguish touched the heart of God. There is a wonderful confidence in this prayer that if God hears, then God will respond.

The psalms remind us that we, too, can take our complaints to God. The psalms teach us how to pray for our needs. The psalms coach us to pray and to believe that God hears our prayers. "In my distress I called upon the Lord. . . . and my cry to him reached his ears."

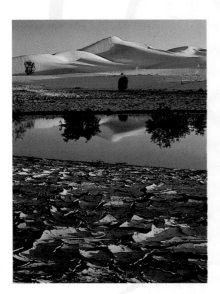

There was a time I was going through a difficult transition in a new job. I was working long hours and not taking time to pray. I ran out of energy. I prayed for help and direction. God's answer came in a letter from a friend. She wrote, "I suspect your greatest teacher will continue to be your own life with its ups and downs, its dry periods and oases. There is something very moving about that. It is so easy to speak of all the grand theories of spirituality; yet our lives often take us to another reality. That other reality shatters the ideal we constantly rebuild of a life full of great experiences of God. Those experiences are sometimes given. But I sometimes think the opposite experiences are the most important, because they bring us out of dependence on our mastery of the spiritual life and throw us in all frailty toward growing dependence on God."

Her letter reminded me that I did not have to have it all together, and that I needed to trust God. It is the simple assurance that God is with us, loves us, and listens to our prayers that really matters.

God is creative in responding to us, using the letter of a friend, a dream, a growing sense of peace, or a sudden insight. God hears and responds to our prayers.

HELP FOR THE BROKENHEARTED

*When the righteous cry for help, the Lord hears,
and rescues them from all their troubles. The Lord is near
to the brokenhearted, and saves the crushed in spirit.*

PSALM 34:17–18

IF ANYONE EVER had a broken spirit, it was David, King of Israel.

He was a rough king in a rough world. In fact, God wouldn't allow him to build the temple because he was a man of war. His kingdom was filled with violence and sorrow. His own son rebelled and tried to take over his kingdom.

And yet he wrote many touching and thoughtful psalms, and his spirit was soft toward God. In fact, the Scriptures even call him a "man after God's own heart."

He had been a devout young man who found both strength and solace in prayer. But as a mighty warrior and a young king, he became arrogant and selfish until his heart was broken, and he then returned to God.

The transformation occurred when he sent his troops off to war. He should have gone with them, for alone in the safety of his palace he saw and then seduced Bathsheba, the wife of one of his soldiers. Then, to cover his sins, he sent orders for her husband to be sent into the front lines and then abandoned.

The Lord sent the prophet Nathan to confront the young king, accusing him of both adultery and murder. "I have sinned against the Lord," David admitted.

"Even so, the son born to you will die," the prophet said.

Sure enough, the baby that had been born to David and Bathsheba became sick, and David spent seven days fasting and praying for the child. David refused to eat or even to bathe. But finally, when the baby died, he got up, washed himself, and worshiped the Lord.

There is no trace of bitterness in his response in a prayer of confession and faith recorded in Psalm 51. He acknowledged his sin, and he asked for forgiveness. And although he could not get his child back, he could get his joy back. "Restore to me the joy of your salvation, and sustain in me a willing spirit," he prayed. "My tongue will sing aloud of your deliverance. O Lord, open my lips, and my mouth will declare your praise" (Psalm 51:12, 14–15).

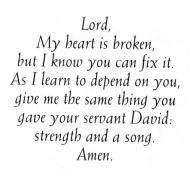

Lord,
My heart is broken,
but I know you can fix it.
As I learn to depend on you,
give me the same thing you
gave your servant David:
strength and a song.
Amen.

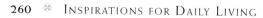

Because of his troubles David understood better who God was and what he wanted. "For you have no delight in sacrifice," he wrote. "The sacrifice acceptable to God is a broken spirit; a broken and contrite heart, O God, you will not despise" (Psalm 51:16–17).

David was still a man of war, a king with many challenges to confront. But he was a kinder and gentler king. Psalm after psalm reflects how in difficulty after difficulty he turned to God. "When the righteous cry for help, the Lord hears, and rescues them in their troubles," he writes. For David this was especially true for the wounded and broken in spirit.

David believed God would comfort them, as he had comforted David himself beside the deathbed of his son. That is not to say there would be no consequences for their actions—but there would be mercy and forgiveness and strength.

That's just exactly what we need to be, men and women "after God's own heart."

SWEET HOUR OF PRAYER

Sweet hour of prayer,
    sweet hour of prayer,
that calls me from a world of care,
and bids me at my Father's throne
make all my wants and wishes known.
In seasons of distress and grief
my soul has often found relief,
and oft escaped the tempter's snare
by your return, sweet hour of prayer.

Sweet hour of prayer,
    sweet hour of prayer,
the joy I feel, the bliss I share,
of those whose anxious spirits burn
with strong desires for your return!
With such I hasten to the place
where God my Savior shows his face,
and gladly take my station there,
and wait for you, sweet hour of prayer.

Sweet hour of prayer,
    sweet hour of prayer,
your wings shall my petition bear

to him whose truth and faithfulness
engage the waiting soul to bless.
And since he bids me seek his face,
believe his Word, and trust his grace,
I'll cast on him my ev'ry care,
and wait for you, sweet hour of prayer.

WILLIAM WALFORD

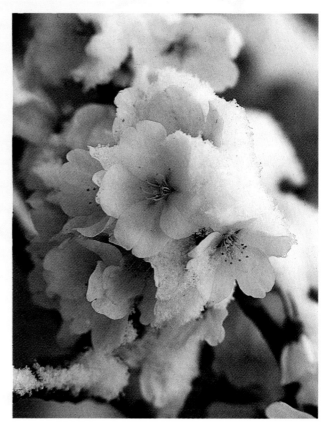

LONG AGO AND FAR AWAY

Hear my cry, O God; listen to my prayer.
From the end of the earth I call to you, when my heart is faint.
Lead me to the rock that is higher than I; for you are
my refuge, a strong tower against the enemy.

PSALM 61:1–3

I WAS HEADED out the door when the phone rang. The machine would get it, I figured, but I paused to hear who it was.

"Hi, it's Faith," the voice crackled. "It's been a long time."

Yes, it had. I had worked with Faith on a project ten years earlier, and we had become close friends. But she'd been living in the big city for a year or two now, and we had lost touch. She met a guy who distracted her from old friendships. She stopped returning calls.

Now, after more than a year of silence, she was reaching out over the phone lines. I had somewhere to be. My hand was on the doorknob. But her voice sounded so plaintive: "I don't know if you want anything to do with me, but I need some help."

I picked up the phone: "Faith, it's great to hear from you! I'm glad you called. What's up?"

There on the phone and over lunch the next day her story unfolded. The guy she loved was indeed bad for her. She was basically addicted to him, and he was addicted to drugs. After being thoroughly used by him, she finally broke off the relationship—and now she needed strength to hold on to that decision. I agreed to help her as best I could.

When Faith called, she was in the place of the psalmist in Psalm 61. He was crying out to God "from the end of the earth." His heart was "faint." He felt very weak and far away from the help he needed.

Maybe you've been there, too. Your relationship with God used to be close, but you've been distracted by other loves. You've let your faith lapse as you've got-

ten yourself into more and more trouble. The tide of life has carried you out to sea, and now you feel as if you're a world away from where you used to be. Would God want anything to do with you anymore? Would he even know your name?

Some get to that point and never cry for help. They're too ashamed to pray, assuming that God would be miffed. But the psalmist assures us that the Lord listens to our prayers even when we're far away. In one famous parable, Jesus pictured God as a loving father watching for the return of his prodigal son. The father spied the boy "while he was still far off" and welcomed him with open arms (Luke 15:20).

Picture the high-powered executive who gets beeped during an important board meeting. Checking the number, he excuses himself to make an important return call to his daughter at home, who needs help with her math homework. God is always on call. Sure, he must have more important things to do, but he lovingly chooses to attend to our needs.

So call him! No matter where you find yourself, no matter how long it's been. God has promised to listen to our prayers. He will take your call.

I don't know of a single foreign product that enters this country untaxed except the answer to prayer.
MARK TWAIN

The Christian on his knees sees more than the philosopher on tiptoe.
DWIGHT L. MOODY

UNDER HIS WINGS

Under his wings I am safely abiding,
though the night deepens and tempests
　　are wild;
still I can trust him, I know he
　　will keep me,
he has redeemed me and I am his child.
Under his wings, under his wings, who
　　from his love can sever?
Under his wings my soul shall abide,
　　safely abide forever.

Under his wings, O what precious
　　enjoyment!
There will I hide till life's trials are o'er;
sheltered, protected,
　　no evil can harm me,
resting in Jesus I'm safe evermore.
Under his wings, under his wings, who
　　from his love can sever?
Under his wings my soul shall abide,
　　safely abide forever.

WILLIAM O. CUSHING

JUST A THOUGHT

The psalmist's world was craggy, full of rocky canyons. David spent his youth as a shepherd saving sheep who had wandered into precarious positions. On occasion, he even had to battle wild animals to rescue them. As a young adult David had to hide in desert caves and scamper through canyons to evade killers. As a warrior he knew the military advantages and disadvantages of this rocky terrain.

Low in these canyons you could fall victim to enemy archers or roving animals. But if you could reach the rocks atop the canyon walls, you'd be safe. In Psalm 61, David asks God to lead him to "the rock that is higher than I," a place of safety and power. In fact, God is that rock, a refuge, a military tower, keeping his people safe from the enemy.

GOD PROMISES ABUNDANT LIFE NOW

And GOD IS ABLE to provide you with every blessing in abundance, so that by always having enough of everything, you may share abundantly in every good work.

2 CORINTHIANS 9:8

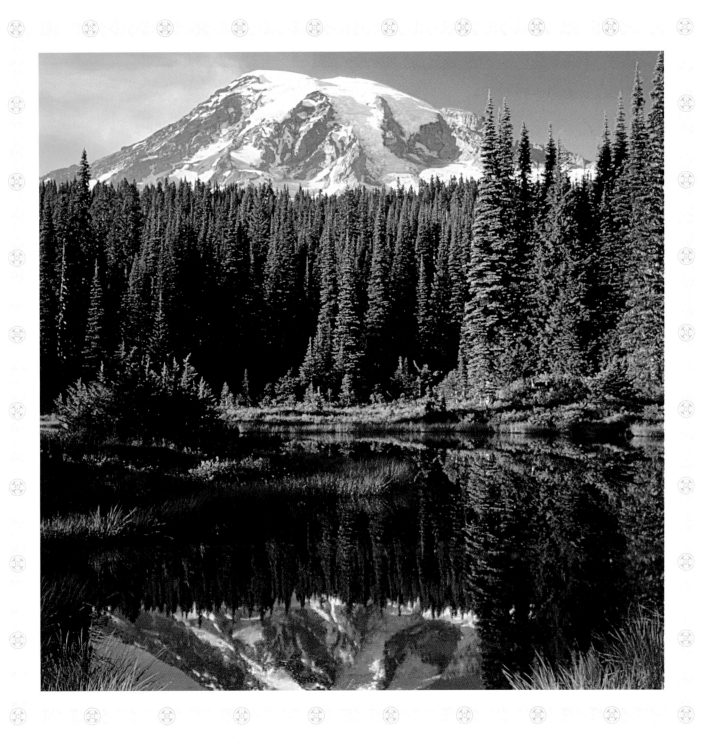

EYES OF A MYSTIC

I came that they may have life, and have it abundantly.

JOHN 10:10

ITCH WAS a wise four-year-old in our church nursery school. He has a wonderful knack for seeing things in a new way and being thrilled with living. One day he called me out of the office, "Hey Wary, [my name is Larry; he wasn't quite getting all the consonants yet] you wanna see me take a drink of water?" I watched him move a stool up to the drinking fountain and take a long drink of water. He was beaming as he finished, like he had just sunk the winning basket in a playoff game.

It was such an ordinary event, yet he filled the moment with a precious simplicity and a contagious joy. I believe Mitch is tuned into the abundant life.

The abundant life is all around us if we have eyes to see. Jesus was not speaking about accumulating great wealth or having many possessions. In fact, Jesus often speaks against such a lifestyle of acquisitions, because it takes one's focus away from God. The stock portfolio, the bigger house, the fancier car begin to matter more

than obedience to a God who desires compassion and sharing, not selfish hearts and hoarding. The encounter that the rich tax collector Zacchaeus had with Jesus reveals the emptiness of a life based on possessions (Luke 19:1–10). Zacchaeus experienced a new freedom when he gave away what he had been clutching so closely. Jesus said that salvation, which could be another word for abundant life, had arrived.

Jesus came to bring a life based on gratitude and blessing. Like Mitch, if we have eyes to see the wonder around us, we will always be led to praise and thanks-

giving. The abundant life has to do with being aware of the miracles around us.

Begin with the miracle of ourselves. Our bodies are wonderful systems of movement, thought, and feeling. When we look into a mirror, we can see the image of God looking back at us. Each day we can experience the joy of touching, tasting, listening, seeing, sitting, and even sleeping. No matter how able-bodied or disabled we may be, we can still feel gratitude for the life that God has given us.

Be aware of the miracle of others, of being in relationships. The abundant life is to enjoy the company of others, to learn more about ourselves as we engage with them. Many have said that if they had to choose possessions or relationships, they would choose to be rich with friends and family. Our circumstances in life may not approach millionaire status, but we can live the abundant life now, with a network of caring friends.

The abundant life Jesus is talking about is focused on seeing the spiritual side of life. God has not only gifted us with bodies and friends, but he invites us to know and experience the presence of the Spirit. God is in us and all around us if we have the eyes to see. Our eyes over a lifetime will bring into focus some 24 billion images. Imagine if all the images that we see are seen through the lens of God's love and presence. Then all of life becomes blessed, and we are living in abundance. It is not only mystics or saints that have this kind of vision, but all of us, living in the awareness of the sacredness of life, who should be overwhelmed with God's abundant grace that is all around us.

There is always the invitation to respond to the life that God offers and to see with new eyes that glory, hope, and blessing are all around us. Even a drink of cool water can be a holy event connecting us to an abundant God.

Everyone who is born into this life comes with the equipment necessary to be a mystic, since we were all created for communion with God. This communing talent that mystics possess is often lost in the passage from childhood (where all is awesome and mystical) into adulthood. Today, 99% of the population has been successfully demystified by education, religious institutions, and the grind of daily life, and so is unable to truly wonder. But mystics, the one percent who hold out—or those who return to childhood— enjoy the prayer of wonder, of being awestruck by the sensation of the Divine Mystery in creation and throughout life. Contrary to popular belief, mystics are not those who have otherworldly visions, but rather those who have visions inside this world.

ED HAYS, *THE OLD HERMIT'S ALMANAC*

ENOUGH TO GO AROUND

For to all those who have, more will be given,
and they will have an abundance.

MATTHEW 25:29

MANAGEMENT GURU Stephen Covey has popularized what he calls a "win-win" mentality. He challenges the cutthroat spirit both behind and even within many businesses, arguing that competitiveness is sometimes unnecessary and unwise.

If this is true, then we don't have to worry when others are successful. In fact, we can be genuinely happy for them. Their success may even increase, rather than diminish, our own. This requires what Covey calls an "abundance mentality."

Leaders who are capable of this kind of thinking are not afraid to share recognition, profits, and responsibility. In fact, they realize that this fosters growth and success. He claims this abundance mentality produces more power, profits, and recognition for everybody.

Unfortunately, many people have a hard time sharing anything, especially credit or power. They have a hard time being happy when others, even their own family and friends, are successful. They hoard things, protecting their own "turf," doing their own thing. They are uncertain and insecure. They are fearful and unhappy. They just don't believe there is enough to go around.

Covey thinks they are wrong. And so did Jesus.

Jesus told the story of a man who went on a long trip and left his three servants with different amounts of money. The two servants with the most went out and invested it, but the one with the least went out and buried it.

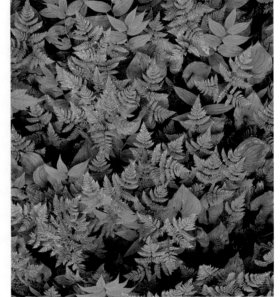

The last servant was not doing something stupid or unusual, however. People often buried their money or jewels to keep them safe from thieves. However, he may have been doing something unwise.

When the master returned, he called his servants together and asked what they had done with his money. The first two had doubled it, and he was pleased. He said, "Well done, good and trustworthy slave; you have been trustworthy in a few things, I will put you in charge of many things; enter into the joy of your master."

But the third servant had nothing to show except the original amount of money. "I was afraid of losing it," he said. The master was unhappy, and he took the money away from him and gave it to the first servant. "You wicked and lazy slave," he said to the third servant. "You ought to have invested my money with the bankers, and on my return I would have received what was my own with interest."

Neither Jesus nor Covey are investment bankers. They are concerned about principles and the spirit. What they are both saying is that there is plenty to go around, and that there isn't any virtue in fearful, self-protective behavior. Trusting others and investing in them may be risky, but it has its rewards. Or, as Jesus put it, "to all those who have, more will be given, and they will have an abundance."

This is a simple principle and a simple promise. Our Master will give us more if we use what we already have in his service. He is not happy when we hoard. But whenever we use what he gives us in his interest, we end up with more and not less. In the kingdom of God, there is always enough to go around.

TAKE MY LIFE, AND LET IT BE CONSECRATED

Take my life, and let it be
consecrated, Lord, to thee;
take my moments and my days,
let them flow in ceaseless praise,
let them flow in ceaseless praise.

Take my hands, and let them move
at the impulse of thy love.
Take my feet, and let them be
swift and beautiful for thee,
swift and beautiful for thee.

Take my love; Lord, I pour
at thy feet its treasure store.
Take myself, and I will be
thine for all eternity,
thine for all eternity.

FRANCIS RIDLEY HAVERGAL

*Lord,
I'm glad that the more I give, you give.
Reward me for the risks I take on your behalf.
Amen.*

TRAVELING LIGHT

Again Jesus spoke to them, saying, "I am the light of the world. Whoever follows me will never walk in darkness but will have the light of life."

JOHN 8:12

HAS THIS EVER happened to you? You find yourself moping, trudging through the dark rooms of your home, depressed for no reason. You're just down. Then you raise the shades, open the blinds, spread the curtains. Or the sun comes out, and you go for a walk. Suddenly it gets bright, and you feel better.

There's a term for this: Seasonally Adjusted Depression (SAD). Seriously! Lots of people get SAD in the middle of winter if they don't live in sunny climes. The cause? Not enough sunlight. Of course, the sun's up for a shorter time in the winter, and during most of those hours we're cooped up indoors. People go to work in the dark and come home in the dark. They can go days without any real sunshine in their lives. No wonder they're depressed!

The solution? Get out of the house! Soak up whatever rays you can! Take a day off and frolic in the park.

Go to Cancun. Or, if that's not feasible, try "light thera-py," which can duplicate the effect of the sun.

Light can have a good effect on us. Lack of light can be a problem. No wonder Jesus used that image to describe himself. He's "the light of the world," bringing warmth and joy, life and vision to everyone who comes to him.

I remember coming home from a weekend trip when I was a teenager. It was late, and, not wanting to wake my parents, I didn't bother to turn on the lights as I walked through the living room. Splat! I tripped over the coffee table. My parents had moved the furniture that weekend.

*The glory of God
is a person fully alive.*
IRENAEUS

Walking in darkness is dangerous.

If you've ever had to walk down a dark, unfamiliar street, you know it's true. You're vulnerable to attack, and who knows what you might stumble over?

Spiritually speaking, the same holds true. Jesus helps us see things as they really are. When we stay close to him, we avoid many of the pitfalls of life. In the bright light of his presence, we can walk safely, we can run, we can dance!

Walk in the light! So you shall know
that fellowship of love.
His Spirit only can bestow,
who reigns in light above.

Walk in the light! And you shall find
your heart made truly his,
who dwells in cloudless light enshrined,
in whom no darkness is.

Walk in the light! And yours shall be
a path, though thorny, bright.
For God, by grace, shall dwell in thee,
and God himself is light.

BERNARD BARTON, ADAPTED

*One person who has mastered
life is better than a thousand
persons who have mastered only
the contents of books, but no
one can get anything out of life
without God.*

MEISTER ECKHARDT

O LOVE THAT WILL NOT LET ME GO

O Light that foll'west all my way,
I yield my flick'ring torch to thee;
my heart restores its borrowed ray,
that in thy sunshine's blaze its day
may brighter, fairer be.

GEORGE MATHESON

SURPRISED BY GRACE

But, as it is written, "No eye has seen, nor ear heard, nor the human heart conceived, what God has prepared for those who love him."

1 CORINTHIANS 2:9

Y SON THINKS it is great fun to hide behind a door or behind a chair and jump out and surprise us. We usually jump, let out a scream, and get mildly annoyed at our beloved child. Yet I do not think that such a surprise is on quite the scale that Paul is talking about.

Most scholars believe that Paul is quoting from chapter 64 of Isaiah, where the prophet is testifying that there is no God like the God of the Israelites. No one has ever seen or heard of a God who does such wonderful deeds for a group of people, who welcomes people who delight in doing what is right. Paul is quoting the prophet to show the Corinthian people that God is truly amazing. Furthermore, Paul can tell them even more about God's love known in Jesus Christ because the Holy Spirit has revealed God's wisdom to Paul.

God is truly surprising, doing what no eye has seen nor ear has heard. Paul isn't talking about a magic act, but about the way God works through Jesus Christ. We have a Sunday at church called Amazing Grace Sunday. It is a day we invite a member of the congregation to tell about God's amazing grace in his or her life. The stories told are filled with trials and pains, addictions and illnesses, but always there is the surprising action of God working for good. At the end of a long bout with drinking or in the middle of brain surgery, one would not expect the story to turn out all right. Yet God is able to do what no eye has seen nor heart has conceived. We always finish the worship service singing "Amazing Grace." That song was written by John Newton, a former captain of a slave-trader ship, who was surprised by the love of God and gave up his slaving days for the chance to tell people about the surprising mercy of God. At that service we celebrate the abundant life that is available to each one of us in surprising ways.

Sometimes we don't trust that God is surprising us with blessings and opportunities. I have a friend who loves the theater. She has taught acting, directed plays, and forever is dreaming of going on stage herself. Not long ago, she was offered a part in a professional production. Yet, instead of being elated, she was nervous and hesitant. She said, "I am afraid of success." She is very talented, and now God has not only blessed her with ability, but he has also blessed and surprised her with an opportunity to use that talent. She is having to work through past experiences of disappointment and rejection so she can trust herself to embrace the abundant life now.

It is important to celebrate the surprising blessings of God. Sometimes we take God's abundant grace for granted, or we are so sure that we know the way that God will act. We lose the ability to see the surprising ways God is at work around us. There are other times we tend to focus on the pains and problems of life. In the old days there were testimonies in churches. I think they went out of fashion when the same folks repeated the same testimonies. They lost their freshness, but the time may be ripe to recover the tradition of brief expressions of God's abundant grace. May we never lose our openness to be surprised by God's love and grace.

You are already surrounded by God ... you do not need to do anything. Let yourself be addressed.

W. PAUL JONES, *THE PROVINCE BEYOND THE RIVER*

AMAZING GRACE

Amazing grace! How sweet the sound
that saved a wretch like me!
I once was lost, but now am found;
was blind, but now I see.

The Lord has promised good to me,
his word my hope secures;
he will my shield and portion be,
as long as life endures.

JOHN NEWTON

HAPPY NEW YEAR

So if anyone is in Christ, there is a new creation:
everything old has passed away; see, everything has become new!

2 CORINTHIANS 5:17

ONE OF THE THINGS I like about being a college professor is that I get two New Years.

The one in January is a lot like everybody else's. I decide to lose weight, be nicer to my mom, give up chocolate. I can make a dozen resolutions and break them all well before February.

Then winter drags on. The sky is gray. My students are surly. I'm becoming cynical and peevish. By April, we're all counting down the days until school is out. I think about what I was trying to do and whether or not I've done it. Papers and projects are piling up on my desk. I'm working long hours, helping with the student newspaper until the wee hours of the morning and completing an endless cycle of administrative reports. I keep wondering if the students are getting it—or if I even know what it is they are supposed to be getting.

Finally, summer comes. The sun shines. I play a little golf. I take a trip. I read a book. I reassess my callings and my commitments. Students who graduated find jobs, get married, and I rejoice in their successes. It all seems worthwhile, and I begin to think about how I can do it better next school year.

Then comes September, and it's New Year again. For some reason, this is a less stressful beginning than the one in January. For one thing, there isn't a tradition of accountability, forcing me to make unreasonable resolutions. But I think the real reason is that everything is new.

New faces. New notebooks. New pencils. New chalk. New books. New energy. New hope. Things look different, smell different, and feel different than they did in May. All my past sins are forgiven. I put on my academic regalia for convocation and march into the new school year as a man with a mission. The calendar year that began so gloomily in January is already two-thirds over, but I get a new start.

Faith is like that. Just when it seems like we've failed, there is some sort of break in our lives, and we realize that Christ is in control. We begin to understand that there are larger purposes than we had imagined, and then, suddenly, everything is new.

God's forgiveness always represents a new beginning. "Everything old has passed away," Paul writes. "See, everything has become new!"

Our life becomes a clean chalkboard again. We have a new song, a new covenant, a new heaven, a new earth, a new way, and a new name. These are just a few of the new things the Scriptures promise.

But the promise that offers us the most hope is a new beginning. We are surrounded with new opportunities. In Christ we have new things to say and new ways to say them. And because God's forgiveness is limitless and free, we can have this experience every day, not just once or twice a year.

❈ ❈ ❈ ❈

Lord,
Thank you for being a God of new beginnings.
Give me a fresh start today as I trust in you.
Amen.

❈ ❈ ❈ ❈

BENEDICTION

What counts is a new creation. Peace and mercy to everyone who follows this rule.

FROM THE EPISTLE TO THE GALATIANS

TIME TO SING!

I will sing to the Lord, because he has dealt bountifully with me.
PSALM 13:6

MUSICAL THEATER can seem unrealistic. If you've watched *Oklahoma!* or *The Sound of Music* or *The King and I* on stage or at the movies, you know what I'm talking about. Two people are chatting away, and suddenly one bursts into song. Imagine if that happened in real life. You're pushing your cart through the supermarket and suddenly the Muzak swells and the cashiers start belting out, "Will you buy our cabbages? Mushrooms and radishes?"

You might look for another place to shop.

I used to make fun of musicals until I realized what they're about. Musicals heighten the emotions of characters until they just have to sing. When you feel super-strongly about something, mere words aren't enough. You must burst into song. Granted, some musicals are pretty corny about this, but they've created a world in which emotions are naturally expressed in music and song.

Is that so strange?

Sometimes you're so happy, you probably find yourself humming or whistling a tune. If you're in the shower where no one can hear you (you hope), you may even perform a concert. If you're in the car with the radio blasting, you may sing along. Even if you're not a singer, you may drum your fingers, clap your hands, or take a few impromptu dance steps during times of high emotion.

That's where the psalmist finds himself in this verse. He has to sing because the Lord has dealt bountifully with him. The Hebrew word for dealing bountifully carries the concept of completeness and then some. God provides what we need, and more. As Paul said in Ephesians 3:20, the Lord "by the power at work within us is able to accomplish abundantly far more than all we can ask or imagine." That's enough to make you want to sing.

Music is the art of the soul . . . one of the most magnificent and delightful presents God has given us.

MARTIN LUTHER

SING PRAISE TO GOD WHO REIGNS ABOVE

Sing praise to God who reigns above,
the God of all creation,
the God of power, the God of love,
the God of our salvation;
with healing balm my soul he fills,
and ev'ry faithless murmur stills:
to God all praise and glory!

The Lord is never far away,
but, thro' all grief distressing,
an ever present help and stay,
our peace and joy and blessing;
as with a mother's tender hand,
he leads his own, his chosen band:
to God all praise and glory!

So all my toilsome way along
I sing aloud thy praises,
that all may hear the grateful song
my voice unwearied raises;
be joyful in the Lord, my heart,
both soul and body, bear your part:
to God all praise and glory!

JOHANN J. SCHÜTZ
TRANSLATED BY FRANCES E. COX

It matters not how long you live, but how well.

PUBLILIUS SYRUS

Let us endeavor so to live that when we come to die even the undertaker will be sorry.

MARK TWAIN

Whate'er my fears or foes suggest,
you are my hope, my joy, my rest.
My heart shall feel your love and raise
my cheerful voice to sing your praise.

ISAAC WATTS

Lord,
You always surprise me with the blessings you give.
My life is full of your joy.
Just when I need a kind word,
A pat on the back,
A helpful push,
You send someone to offer it.
You find a million ways to let me know you love me.

Lord,

I want to sing a Hallelujah Chorus.

I want to gather all my neighbors into a choir

To sing out how wonderful you are.

Even that wouldn't do justice to your sweet mercy.

But I'll find my ways to praise you

As I go through my days.

I'll send tiny hallelujahs skyward,

I'll sing quiet anthems in my car, in my garden.

Lord,

I thank you for your kindness.

My life is full of you.

GOD PROMISES ETERNAL LIFE LATER

BLESSED BE the God and Father of our Lord Jesus Christ! By his great mercy he has given us a new birth into a living hope through the resurrection of Jesus Christ from the dead, and into an inheritance that is imperishable, undefiled, and unfading, kept in heaven for you.

1 PETER 1:3–4

FAMILIAR WORDS, WONDERFUL PROMISES

For God so loved the world that he gave his only Son, so that everyone who believes in him may not perish but may have eternal life. Indeed, God did not send the Son into the world to condemn the world, but in order that the world might be saved through him.

JOHN 3:16–17

OR MANY PEOPLE, myself included, the first Bible verse ever memorized was John 3:16. I can remember sitting in the basement of my home church trying to memorize various Bible verses. The one that remains is John 3:16. It is such a pivotal verse in the Bible and seems to have entered American culture as a summary of Christian faith. Often at a sporting event you can see someone holding up a sign with just the words "John 3:16." The verse seems to be everywhere, but its familiarity should not breed contempt or neglect.

The verse is part of a dialogue between Jesus and a pharisee named Nicodemus, a leader of the Jews. The dialogue is held in the quiet of the night, perhaps so Nicodemus won't be seen going to Jesus. Yet he is gen-

uinely interested in the message that Jesus has been teaching. The dialogue takes some different twists and leaves Nicodemus wondering about how to be born from above, how to be born anew. Jesus is taking Nicodemus into some deeper understandings of faith and life. It is not so much the physical that can be seen, but the spiritual, which is as invisible and yet still as noticeable as the wind. Jesus invites Nicodemus to be aware of the movement of the Spirit and to receive its insights.

Jesus is pointing Nicodemus and us to the incredible love of God. A love so big it reaches out to embrace the whole world; a love so deep that God is willing to risk sending the son to show us salvation.

This is a passage about love and God's intentions that all might be saved, that all might know the tender embrace of God in life and in life beyond death. It is sad that sometimes what comes out of churches today is judgment and condemnation. It is as though churches have forgotten to read verse 17, "God did not send the son into the world to condemn the world." It is so easy to be judgmental and critical. It is so easy to point out another person's faults, another nation's errors.

In the history of Christianity there has been far too much blood spilled by Christians who took condemnation and separateness too far. We should ask one another's forgiveness for losing track of the central theme of God's love—God was willing to let Jesus die so we might see the power of sacrificial love.

In Jesus' death and resurrection, he became the risen Christ. The risen Christ is not bound by human limitations but is free to be known in all times and places. The risen Christ shows us the path to eternal life.

Several years ago, while on a wilderness prayer retreat, I had some prayer dialogues with the risen Christ. In the prayer, I felt like the risen Christ knew my struggles and questions. I heard words of reassurance, "I know what you are going through. None of us received all the love we needed from our parents. I will be with you. I am as close to you as your breath." The conversations renewed a relationship with Jesus, who is still present to us as the risen Christ, crossing all boundaries of time and space. Such moments in prayer are a foretaste of eternal life, which is present in our daily lives if we but look. The communion with Christ is a taste of what is to come, for neither life nor death, nor things present, nor things to come can separate us from the love of God in Christ Jesus our Lord (see Romans 8:31–39).

Indeed, John 3:16–17 serves as an important reminder that God's will is for all people to come into a relationship with God. Jesus is the avenue to that homecoming, the risen Christ is the pathway to eternal life. St. Augustine said it wisely, "Our hearts are restless till they find their rest in God." Thanks for these verses and their promise.

Lord God,

Your love is deeper than the deepest sea.

Your love is higher than the highest star in heaven.

Your grace to me is free—another unmatchable gift
from you to me.

Give me thankfulness for your mercy.

Give me gratitude for your love.

Give me an appreciation of all your gifts—so freely
given to one as undeserving as me.

THE WATER OF LIFE

*Those who drink of the water that I will give them will
never be thirsty. The water that I will give will become in
them a spring of water gushing up to eternal life.*

JOHN 4:14

I'VE NEVER BEEN in the desert, but I have been really thirsty. It was last spring, during a rather stressful time in my life. I was tired all the time and losing weight. And I was really, really thirsty—all the time.

I remember going to a conference in Alexandria, Virginia, and walking along the river with a friend. In just a short walk, I stopped in two different stores to buy bottled water. And at a meeting in Grand Rapids, Michigan, I borrowed a car from a colleague one evening and went to the store for a gallon of water—and drank it all in less than an hour.

I didn't know why I was thirsty at the time, or even what I was thirsting for. As it turned out, I had adult onset diabetes. And once I got it under control, my unquenchable thirst became more manageable. But I can remember craving water like I used to crave chocolate, wanting a drink more than anything I had ever wanted.

We have a similar thirst for God, what Blaise Pascal called "a God shaped vacuum in the heart of every man which cannot be filled by any created thing." We long for lots of things, but one of the things we long for— without even knowing how or why—is a long cool drink from the reservoir of God's grace.

Jesus knew we had this thirst. And he knew just what would satisfy it.

Water, of course, was a precious commodity in the dry, rocky hills of Palestine. But at Jacob's well, Jesus told the Samaritan woman—a social out- cast—that he could give her a drink so satisfying that she would never thirst again. In fact, he would give her a whole spring—gushing up to eternal life. There is no doubt that the water Jesus offered was himself. He told his disciples that "whoever believes in me will never be thirsty" (John 6:35).

Later, in Jerusalem for the Feast of Tabernacles, Jesus watched as the priests performed an elaborate ritual, carrying water from the Pool of Siloam to a silver basin next to the altar. Each morning for a week the water

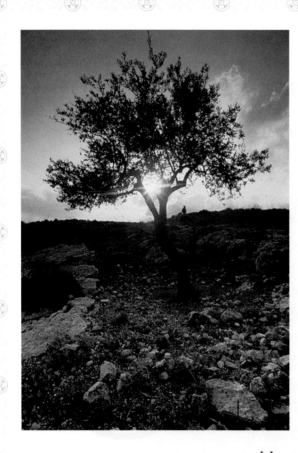

was brought up in a solemn fashion, accompanied by priests blowing trumpets and waving bundles of willow branches. The priests marched around the altar, and then one priest would climb the ramp to the altar, lift a bowl high above the crowd, and then pour the precious water onto the altar as a sacrifice.

On the last day of the feast, the priests marched around the altar seven times, beating the ground with the willows. And then, as the priest lifted the bowl, a loud cry came out of the audience. It was Jesus. "Let anyone who is thirsty come to me, and let the one who believes in me drink," he cried (John 7:37–38).

He offered them—and us—a drink to satisfy the diabetes of the soul, a refreshing drink that not only satisfies but cures, not only now but for eternity. The Book of Revelation concludes its description of the delights of heaven this way: "Let everyone who is thirsty come. Let anyone who wishes take the water of life as a gift" (verse 17).

Nothing else can satisfy our soul.

Lord,
I gladly come to the wellspring
of life. Satisfy my thirst,
now and forever.
Amen.

BREAD FOR LIVING

Very truly, I tell you, whoever believes has eternal life. I am the bread of life. Your ancestors ate the manna in the wilderness, and they died. This is the bread that comes down from heaven, so that one may eat of it and not die. I am the living bread that came down from heaven. Whoever eats of this bread will live forever; and the bread that I will give for the life of the world is my flesh.

JOHN 6:47–51

EVERY WEEK, it seems, they're coming up with some new cure for what ails us. New chemicals, ancient herbs—just pop this pill and you'll feel fine, they say. Feeling run-down? Low on energy? Ginseng or St. John's wort or high-protein pasta—something is bound to give you the gumption to get up and go.

Who knows if those things really work? But the basic idea is valid—you are what you eat. Food is our fuel, and if you're sputtering and tired, maybe you need to change your fuel.

Jesus had the same idea—only in his day, they didn't know about vitamins. Bread was the basic fuel. When Jesus told his friends to pray for their daily bread, it wasn't just something to smear peanut butter and jelly on. Bread itself fueled them until the next day.

God provides our daily bread, and we thank him for it. In the desert, he rained manna on the wandering Israelites. The word "manna" in Hebrew means, "What is it?"—something they must have wondered as they stepped over the morsels that first morning. But those who tried to whip up some manna leftovers discovered something interesting. It wouldn't keep. Their daily bread lasted for a day, and then it spoiled. Every new day they had to count on God.

That is the backdrop for Jesus' amazing promise in John 6. He identifies himself as "bread that comes down from heaven"—just like the manna. But there's an important difference. Manna spoiled; Jesus lasts forever. If our life journey is going to take us to the next world, we need more than daily bread. We need provisions that will last, bread that will never go stale. And Jesus said he was that bread. Living bread. Bread that imparts life to its eaters, but also bread that is living itself and just as fresh tomorrow as it is today.

How do we eat this bread? Jesus made it clear that the bread was his flesh, so it has something to do with

Surely goodness and mercy shall follow me all the days of my life: and I will dwell in the house of the Lord forever.
PSALM 23:6, KJV

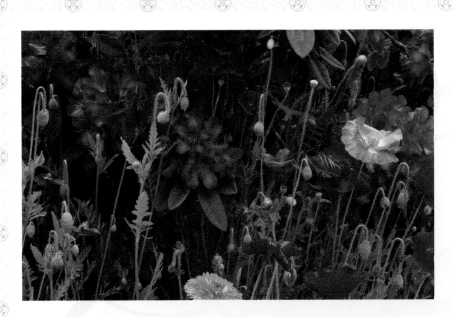

his sacrificial death. But let's not start bickering about eucharistic theology. "Whoever believes has eternal life," he says, and in Scripture believing is trusting, entrusting. When you eat something, you commit yourself to it. You make it part of yourself, counting on it to do you good and not harm.

And that's how we get eternal life—by committing ourselves to Jesus, making him a part of us.

Bread, anyone?

Every saint in heaven is as a flower in the garden of God, and every soul there is as a note in some concert of delightful music.
JONATHAN EDWARDS

LIVING ON IN GOD'S MEMORY

*Jesus said to her, "I am the resurrection and the life.
Those who believe in me, even though they die, will live,
and everyone who lives and believes in me will never die."*

JOHN 11:25–26

EATH IS A MYSTERY. Though we have heard about near-death experiences where people report they go through a tunnel into a glorious, peaceful white light, we still do not have people coming back from death and telling us about the afterlife. How long we live, the circumstances of death, and the details of eternity are a mystery.

Mary and Martha are caught up in that mystery of death in the eleventh chapter of John. Their brother, Lazarus, has just died, and their dear friend Jesus had not come until after his death. They are overcome with grief, yet Jesus announces that God's love is visible in the son, who is "the resurrection and the life." To believe in God is to know a power stronger than death. Death may still be a mystery, but we know who holds the mystery.

Jesus says there is a life that goes on beyond death. One way of understanding that is to know that what we have said and done lives on in the memories and lives of those we have left behind. On All Saints Day, at our church, we remember those who have died in the past year. As each name is read the congregation responds, *"presente,"* which is a Spanish word meaning "they are present with us." In this way, the departed live on in our memories.

There is also a sense that we live on in God's presence. Whatever picture we have of the afterlife, each one points to a God whose love for us does not end at our death. God's love is stronger than any of our tragedies. Jesus promises a full life while we are living and a new life in the resurrection to eternal life. In this way we live on in the presence of God.

After Jesus spoke this verse to Martha, he went to the tomb and raised Lazarus. We, too, have the promise of being raised to eternal life.

ON OUR WAY REJOICING

On our way rejoicing gladly let us go.
Christ our Lord has conquered; vanquished is the foe.
Christ without, our safety; Christ within, our joy;
who, if we be faithful, can our hope destroy?
On our way rejoicing; as we forward move,
hearken to our praises, O blest God of love!

Unto God the Father joyful songs we sing;
unto God the Savior thankful hearts we bring;
unto God the Spirit bow we and adore,
on our way rejoicing now and evermore.
On our way rejoicing; as we forward move,
hearken to our praises, O blest God of love!

JOHN S. B. MONSELL

A HEAVENLY HONEYMOON

"In my father's house there are many dwelling places. If it were not so, would I have told you that I go to prepare a place for you? And if I go to prepare a place for you, I will come again and will take you to myself, so that where I am, there you may be also. And you know the way to the place where I am going." Thomas said to him, "Lord, we do not know where you are going. How can we know the way?" Jesus said to him, "I am the way, and the truth, and the life. No one comes to the Father except through me."

JOHN 14:2–6

THE STORY IS TOLD of a young man in upstate New York whose parents died when he was a teenager, leaving him with a vast fortune. As the young man came of age, he was highly sought after by many young women of social eminence.

So he devised a plan to find a bride who would love him for who he was—not what he had. He left home and took a train to Alabama, carrying only some working clothes in a cardboard suitcase.

He finally found a job in a factory, but he had never worked with his hands before. He was clumsy and awkward, and a young woman at the next table took pity on him. She showed him what to do and how to do it, helping him adjust to an uncomfortable situation.

He found her interesting and attractive. After a while, he explained that he had no folks, and he asked if he could visit with her family. She asked her parents, who were both invalids, and they invited the young man into their home.

She was working to support both her parents. She was industrious and had a pure heart. The young man fell in love with her and began to court her. After several months, he asked her father for permission to marry her. The father gave his consent, and the young woman said yes. She loved him deeply and looked forward to becoming his wife.

The couple wanted to do something special for their honeymoon, so they saved up enough money to buy a train tickets to New York City. And finally, they boarded the train for the long trip north.

She had never left home before, and she was somewhat overwhelmed by Grand Central Station. And then, when they walked outside, a man in a uniform came up and picked up their suitcases.

   "Stop him," she said to her husband. "That man is taking our luggage." But her husband assured her that it was all right. "It's just something special I want to do for you," he told her. And so, somewhat suspiciously, she followed the man with their bags to a limousine.

   "Oh, we can't afford this," she protested.

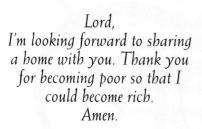

Lord,
I'm looking forward to sharing
a home with you. Thank you
for becoming poor so that I
could become rich.
Amen.

"It's okay," he said. "It's just something special I want to do for you."

So they rode far out into the country and turned finally into a fenced estate, following a long, winding, tree-lined drive to the front of a palatial mansion. Now she knew they were well beyond their meager means, but he insisted everything would be okay. "Get out of the car," he said. "I have something I want to show you."

And then, on the porch, he pulled a key from his pocket, unlocked the door, and carried his bride across the threshold of her new home.

"This is yours," he said. "I have everything you need, and everything your parents need. You thought I was just a poor orphan, but I'm the heir to all this, and I want to share it with you."

Someday the same thing will happen to the Church, which the Bible calls the Bride of Christ. Jesus will sweep us off our feet and carry us across the threshold of his heavenly estate. "You thought I was just a poor Nazarene carpenter," he will say. "But I'm the heir to all this, and I want to share it with you."

"It's just something special I want to do for you."

MY SAVIOR FIRST OF ALL

When my life-work is ended,
    and I cross the swelling tide,
when the bright and glorious
    morning I shall see,
I shall know my Redeemer when
    I reach the other side,
and his smile will be the first to
    welcome me.

Oh, the soul thrilling rapture when I
    view his blessed face,
and the luster of his kindly beaming eye!
How my full soul shall praise him for the
    mercy, love, and grace
that prepare for me a mansion in the sky.

Through the gates to the city in a robe
    of spotless white,
he will lead me where no tears
    shall ever fall.
In the glad songs of ages I shall mingle with delight;
but I long to meet my Savior first of all.

FANNY CROSBY

Changing Times

Listen, I will tell you a mystery! We will not all die, but we will all be changed, in a moment, in the twinkling of an eye, at the last trumpet. For the trumpet will sound, and the dead will be raised imperishable, and we will be changed. For this perishable body must put on imperishability, and this mortal body must put on immortality. When this perishable body puts on imperishability, and this mortal body puts on immortality, then the saying that is written will be fulfilled: "Death has been swallowed up in victory."

1 Corinthians 15:51–54

 NDREA LOVES this verse. She can't wait for the day her "mortal body puts on immortality." You see, she's always been overweight. No amount of exercise or dieting has been able to change her appearance much. She hates her body. Self-esteem books don't help. Encouraging words of friends and family don't matter. Andrea still hates her body—but she knows she's going to get a new one. And she longs for that day more than any teenager awaiting a driver's license. "We will all be changed" is music to her ears, and she listens for that trumpet call.

Maybe that strikes a chord with you, too. You may or may not be satisfied with your body—that's not the point here—but whatever shape you're in, your physical body still holds you back. We're mortal. From the moment the doctor delivers you and hands you to your mother, you are headed on the road toward death. It may take 90 years or more, but your body is perishable. Humanity is a terminal disease.

We're not trying to be macabre here. Human life is a wonderful adventure. Those who know Jesus have abundant life teeming with surprise and delight. And we offer our physical bodies, such as they are, in the worship and service of God. But our bodies, like the rest of the physical universe, are still locked in a process of decay. They are as perishable as the avocados at your local fruit stand—except it takes longer for us to get mushy.

This sobering reality makes today's promise all the more joyful. When Christ comes again, everything changes. We will unzip our bodies like ratty windbreakers and put on exciting new physiques. We don't know much about them except that they're imperishable, not subject to the laws of decay. Maybe they'll be like the body Jesus had after his resurrection—solid, touchable, but able to move through locked doors—or the radiant bodies he, Moses, and Elijah had on the Mount of Transfiguration. Who knows? But we will all be changed.

Our bodies also have this habit of leading us into sin. Lust, anger, selfishness, and sloth all seem to start with our physical urges. Another great thing about our new, improved bodies will be their total devotion to the Lord. They will be immortal and no longer subject to the deeds of sin and death. And whether you're short or tall, fat or thin, a supermodel or a couch potato, that's something to look forward to!

IN HEAVEN ABOVE

In heav'n above, in heav'n above,
where God our Father dwells,
how boundless there the blessedness!
No tongue its greatness tells.
There face to face, and full and free,
the ever living God we see—
our God, the Lord of hosts!

In heav'n above, in heav'n above,
what glory deep and bright!
The splendor of the noonday sun
grows pale before its light:
The heav'nly light that ne'er goes down,
around whose radiance clouds ne'er frown,
is God, the Lord of hosts!

In heav'n above, in heav'n above,
no tears of pain are shed,
for nothing there can fade or die—
life's fullness round is spread;
and, like an ocean, joy o'er flows,
and with immortal mercy glows
our God, the Lord of hosts!

In heav'n above, in heav'n above,
God has a joy prepared
which mortal ear has never heard
nor mortal vision shared,
which ever entered mortal breast,
by mortal lips was n'er expressed:
'tis God, the Lord of hosts!

LAURENTIUS L. LAURINUS, ALT., JOHN ÅSTROM,
TRANSLATED BY WILLIAM MACCALL

TOPICAL INDEX